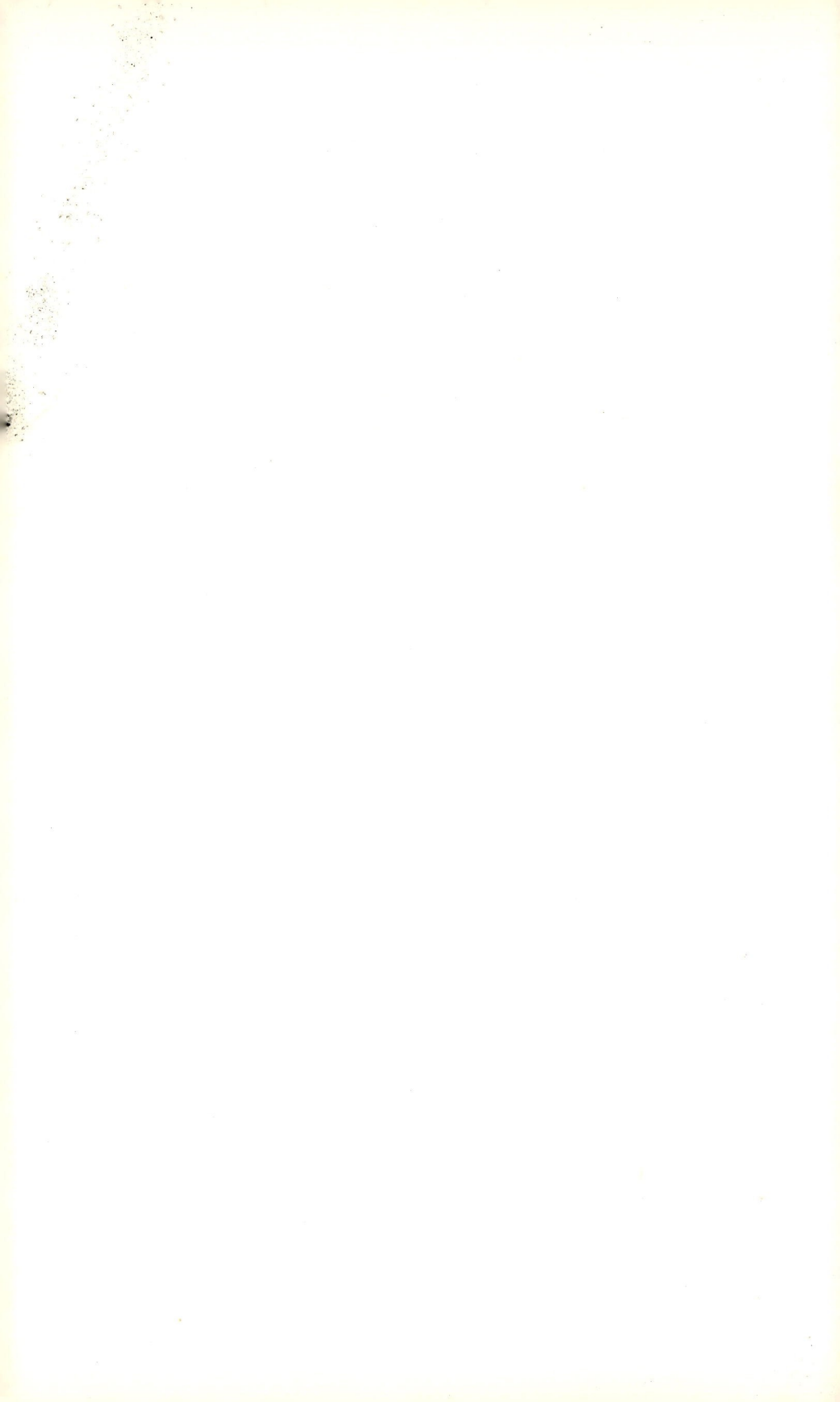

A Thumbnail

History

of

The City of
Houston, Texas

From Its Founding in 1836 to the Year 1912

By Dr. S. O. Young

Copano Bay Press

2010

Originally published in June 1912 under the same title by
Rein & Sons Company of Houston

New material copyright 2010 Copano Bay Press

ISBN: 978-0-9822467-4-0

TABLE OF CONTENTS

An Introduction
By Mark Pusateri

When S. O. Young wrote this book, he was sixty-four. His subject, Houston, was but seventy-six years old. In three quarters of a century, it had grown from a population of 12 to over 80,000. There had been earlier books published on the history of the Bayou City, but most were "mug books" which featured glowing biographies of prominent men, published be sold to those same prominent men. Dr. Young set out to fill a need for a serious history, a sober recording of the facts regarding Houston's development. He poured over original documents in the city and county archives. He further made extensive use of old newspapers housed in Houston's Carnegie Library.

1912 was a landmark year. It can be seen as the cusp of Houston's transformation from a city of regional importance to a national commercial center. Dredging had been finished on the ship channel, prompting city boosters to adopt the slogan: "Where seventeen railroads meet the sea." The Rice Institute (now Rice University) was set to open. The current Harris County Courthouse had just been completed and Jesse Jones was building the Rice Hotel. There was a new city auditorium on the site where Jones Hall now stands. Lumber was booming and, while cotton was still king, oil had all but taken the crown.

Samuel Oliver Young, Jr. (1848-1926) was a native Houstonian. He was born just two months after the death of his father in the midst of a Yellow Fever epidemic. He grew up among veterans of San Jacinto and the most prominent citizens of early Houston. His mother reared him in the home of her father, Nathan Fuller, one of Houston's early mayors. Young served in the Civil War, enlisting as teenager in the Bayou City Guards (Company A, Fifth Texas Infantry), a unit of Hood's Texas Brigade. Like his father before him, S. O. Young became a physician, practicing from 1870 until 1882, when he abandoned medicine to become a newspaperman.

Some readers will already know S. O. Young from his account of the 1900 Galveston Storm which is detailed in Erik Larson's book, *Isaac's Storm*. He was Secretary of the Galveston Cotton Exchange at the time and was determined to ride out the storm in his house. The storm destroyed the house leaving Dr. Young to surf across the island on his front door.

Dr. Young had grown up with Houston. It's history was his history and he presents it within these pages in detail and with pride.

A Word in Advance

In presenting this little volume to the people of Houston for their consideration, I feel that a word of explanation is due. I wrote the book to supply a badly needed "need," of course, but I wrote it more for my own pleasure than for anything else. I have made no attempt at fine writing and have given no thought to literary excellence. My sole object has been to attain accuracy, and every precaution has been taken to guard against error. Wherever possible I have consulted original documents and newspapers. Yet, in spite of this, I fear that some errors have crept in and that the readers will find many statements which they may think erroneous. I say this because there are some stories and traditions that have been repeated so often that many suppose them to be true.

If the readers derive as much pleasure from perusing these pages as I have from writing them, I shall feel content. I have enjoyed writing every line, and add "The End" with regret.

S. O. YOUNG

Houston, June 5, 1912

TO THE MEMORY OF MY MOTHER
MRS. MAUD JEANNIE YOUNG,

whose life was largely devoted to the cause of education and to the creation of a taste for literature and the sciences in the minds of the earlier citizens of Houston, this little volume is lovingly dedicated.

—THE AUTHOR

CHAPTER I:
FOUNDING & GOVERNING A GREAT CITY

A fact not generally known nor appreciated is that Houston is the result of a disagreement between the Allens and the Harrises. There was no serious quarrel or anything of that sort. They simply differed about land matters, with the result that the Allens, instead of joining the Harrises in their efforts to build up the already established town of Harrisburg, came five miles by land and about sixteen miles by water further up the bayou, and laid the foundation for the rival town, which was destined to become the greatest city in Texas and one of the greatest in the Southwest.

Now, as a matter of fact, there was no good reason for the new town. The location at Harrisburg was ideal and had many advantages, naturally, that Houston had to create artificially. There was, to begin with, sixteen miles of very crooked and hardly navigable bayou to be overcome in order to reach Houston, while the new site had absolutely nothing to compensate for this disadvantage.

However, there was an element injected into the controversy that helped the Allens wonderfully in carrying out their scheme. Santa Anna's soldiers showed up just at the critical moment and burned Harrisburg. Before the Harrises could recover from the blow, and while their town still lay in ashes, the Allens acted and not only had their town laid out, but were actively engaged in selling town lots to settlers. Not much progress was made during the first year, however, and there was not much of a city in evidence and scarcely more to indicate where that city was to be.

Governor Frank Lubbock, in his memoirs, gives an amusing description of his search for the town, even after he had reached and passed the foot of Main Street. He came to Houston on the first steamboat that ever arrived here and it took four days to make the trip from Harrisburg to Houston. That being the pioneer trip, an immense amount of work had to be done to clear the stream of sunken logs and overhanging trees. There was plenty of water, but there were numerous obstructions in and over the channel. After that first boat there was little or no delay, and before long there were other boats that came to Houston. In a year or two there was a regular service established between Houston and Galveston.

The question of transportation was one of the most serious with which the early settlers had to contend. Transportation by land was not only difficult, but actually dangerous, for there were hostile Indians and predatory bands of Mexicans ever on the watch for unwary settlers. There were no roads, ordinary trails being the only guides for the traveller, and therefore when communication was established with the outside world by water from Houston, it was looked on as a blessing, since it saved many miles of difficult and dangerous travel. The bayou soon became popular and Houston sprang at once into the greatest prominence as a receiving and distributing point. It is remarkable that Houston should have had all those advantages, and that in the early days and then after the lapse of many years she should still retain them through the commercial activity and business foresight of her citizens.

During the first eighteen months of the new city's existence there was little accomplished aside from perfecting the plans and arranging the divisions of Houston, for there was not much more of a city than a name and some surveyed streets and lots until late in 1837. By then the town began to show some life and activity. It is true that the city was more like a military camp than anything else, for it was composed largely of tents, with here and there a small log cabin. During 1837 there was a large storehouse built at the corner of Commerce Street and Main and at the same time work was begun on the Mansion House, Houston's first hotel. This was located on the corner now occupied by the Southern Pacific offices.

But it was not until 1838 that Houston took on genuine city airs. That year an election was held to decide whether the city should be incorporated or not. The result was an affirmative vote and the same year the Texas Congress granted the City of Houston a charter. Having become a chartered city, it was necessary for Houston to elect a mayor and board of aldermen. Unfortunately all the records of the city have been twice destroyed by fire, but tradition and the oldest inhabitants declare that Dr. Francis Moore, Jr., was the first mayor of Houston.

Now there is really no good nor substantial reason for doubting that Dr. Moore was the first mayor, and the question is brought up in this way so as to give place to a doubt introduced by Maj. Ingham Roberts, who has made a close study of all that relates to the early history of Houston. Major Roberts, in the *History of Southeast Texas*, of which he was one of the editors, publishes a list of Houston's mayors and gives the honor of being the first to James S. Holman. The Major gives as his authority for doing this, a notice published in the *Telegraph* of Sept. 29, 1837, calling an election to fill

A.C. ALLEN Co-FOUNDER of HOUSTON

CHARLOTTE M. ALLEN WIFE OF A.C. ALLEN

JOHN K.ALLEN FOUNDER of HOUSTON.

S. L. ALLEN BROTHER OF J.K. & A.C. ALLEN AND A PIONEER & PATRIOT OF HOUSTON

MRS. S. L. ALLEN WIFE OF S.L.ALLEN.

vacancies caused by the deaths of two aldermen, which notice was signed Jas. S. Holman, "Mayor."

Major Roberts is a most careful student and accurate writer, and yet one is constrained to believe that a serious error has been committed by himself or by the paper publishing that notice. In the first place, Houston was not incorporated until a year after the date of that notice and, therefore, could not have had a mayor or board of aldermen. In the next place, James S. Holman was clerk of the Eleventh District Court from February 1837 until 1842, and it is not likely that he could have been mayor of Houston at the same time. As a matter of fact he was clerk of the court at the very time that notice was published, as the court records show. The matter is given space here so as to bring out all the facts for the guidance of future historians.

When the Moore administration took office, its first act was to extend the city limits, which to that time had been the bayou on the north, Walker Street on the south, Bagby Street on the west and Caroline on the east. The limits were extended so as to embrace nine square miles. This was done in order to increase the taxable area and to include within the city limits many citizens who had built residences just beyond the old city lines. The nine mile area was maintained many years, or until the city fell in the hands of the carpetbag Republicans appointed by E. J. Davis during Reconstruction. They found it necessary, in order to create more plunder, to increase the taxable area so as to embrace twenty-five square miles. When the carpetbaggers were turned out of office by the home people who had regained control of affairs, the city limits were reduced again to nine square miles. That was in 1874, and until 1903 no change was made. But by that time the city had so extended beyond its limits that an increase was demanded in justice and fairness to all, so the area was fixed at sixteen square miles. A remarkable feature is that since those limits were fixed, the city has again far outgrown its bounds, so that a very large number, perhaps 15,000 or 20,000 nominal citizens of Houston are living outside the city limits.

Aside from fixing the city limits and placing some pine trees across the streets, so that people could get across from one corner to another without bogging down in the mud, there appears to have been nothing accomplished by the Moore administration, or by that of G. W. Lively, the second mayor.

It was reserved for the Charles Biglow administration, in 1840, to take the first step towards permanent public improvement. That year, a contract was let for the erection of a market house and city hall on Market Square. That old market was pointed to with pride for many years by all Houstonians. It was really a pretentious building for it had length, if not height, being only a single story high. It extended from Preston to Congress and on the Congress side it was two stories high. The upper floor was used as a city hall, while the lower one was devoted to a city jail or "calaboose."

The market part was given over to the butchers and vegetable people, who had stalls arranged on each side, while a broad alley extended down the entire length of the market. There was no floor, only the bare earth serving for that purpose. The building soon became famous for the number of rats that took possession of it. Perhaps, in no part of the world were there ever so many rats gathered together in a limited space as were found in that old place. However, it was a great improvement on conditions that had prevailed to that time, for the market vendors had been forced to do business in the open air, or under a dilapidated shed that someone had erected. There was a tent, not on the square, however, that was used for market purposes, but that was a private affair with which the city had nothing to do.

The old market house stood for many years and was finally torn down to make place for the famous market house erected by the Scanlan administration. The story of that famous building is worth telling.

Mr. Alexander McGowan had been elected mayor of the city in 1867, but was turned out of office by E. J. Davis, the Reconstruction Governor of Texas, in August, 1868. Some other changes were made, but it was not until 1870, that Davis showed his hand by turning everybody out of office and appointing his own henchmen.

T. H. Scanlan was appointed mayor and four ignorant negroes were made aldermen by Davis. Then the plundering began in real earnest, and by the time they got through Houston had a debt of almost two million dollars and had but little or nothing to show for it. It was no public spirit or local pride that gave Houston the finest market house in the South. Houston got the building finally, but Houston paid a fancy price for it. It was merely the opportunity to extend the loot field that lay behind the market that resulted in its final construction.

Having decided to erect a market house, plans were drawn, specifications made and bids were invited. Col. William Brady was the successful bidder at $250,000. He was backed by some New Yorkers. He agreed to take the city's bonds in payment, the bonds to bear 8 per cent interest and to run twenty-five years. That part of the contract was alright, perhaps, but after actual construction of the building began, things began to show up that were never expected. Col. Brady built according to the plans and specifications, but when those were examined it was found that they contained no provision for blinds, some doors, and in one or two instances, for floors for the building. The whole thing was found to be merely an outline of plans and specifications, but Col. Brady claimed it was what he had bid on and he held the city strictly to its contract with him.

There was only one thing to do—issue more bonds—and that was when the city limits were extended, so as to take in more taxpayers. The tax area was increased, more bonds were issued, and before the market house was completed its total cost was $470,000 instead of $250,000 as originally contemplated. The building was insured for $100,000, but when it was burned down in 1876, the insurance companies refused to pay even that, and, after much haggling, finally agreed to restore the building, which they did at an outlay of only $80,000. The restored building was also destroyed by fire some years later, after which the present magnificent building was erected.

A so-called election was held in 1872, and by importing negroes from the surrounding counties and obstructing the white voters, the Republicans were able to elect the entire city ticket and keep the same gang in office. Retribution was near at hand, however, for the next year the Democrats swept the State and elected Coke Governor. In January, 1874, Houston was granted a new charter by provision of which the Governor was authorized to appoint the city officials of Houston. Governor Coke lost no time, but turned the Scanlan crowd out of office. He then appointed Mr. Jas. T. D. Wilson, mayor, and also appointed a board of aldermen composed of respectable and prominent citizens. A few months later an election was held and all the gentlemen appointed by the Governor were regularly elected.

There was little accomplished by the new administration during their tenure of office. The affairs of the city were so badly tangled and the bonded and floating debts were so large that the city was absolutely without money or credit. Under conditions such as these it was not expected that anything could be done beyond staving off clamoring creditors and answering court summonses, for the city was being constantly sued.

After holding office for one year the Wilson administration retired and Mr. I. C. Lord was chosen as mayor in 1875. He had all that his predecessor had to contend with, and in addition there came up the question of disposing of the interest the city had acquired, in some way, in the Houston East & West Texas Railroad. The interest owned by the city was in that part of the road surveyed as far west as the Brazos near Bellville, but which had been abandoned and has never been built. There were suits and counter-suits and the whole question became very much involved. Finally the city sold its interest for $35,000 and went out of the railroad business for good. But it was a case of jumping out of the frying pan into the fire, for so soon as it was known that the Lord administration had a little cash on hand the courthouse feature became aggravated and everybody was clamoring to get hold of it. Old notes, old and new claims, popped up from unexpected quarters and the situation became desperate. Mr. Lord held office for two years and then quit in disgust.

Mr. Wilson, having had a two years rest, was persuaded by the citizens to try his hand again. This was literally true for at that time a man had to be talked into taking such an onerous office as that of the debt-burdened city. It required patience, honesty of purpose and fine executive and financial ability to keep the affairs of the city going, even for a day, and those who were qualified to act were not anxious to do so.

The second administration of Mr. Wilson resulted in the establishment, or rather in the inauguration of the movement that resulted in establishing the water works here. Before that time Houston depended entirely on underground cisterns for its water supply, both for drinking and for fire protection purposes. Soon after the beginning of his second term, Mr. Wilson sent a special message to the council drawing attention to the great need of water works. The city had no money to build such works, but was prepared and willing to deal most liberally with any private company or corporation that would undertake the work.

Nearly a year later such a company was formed, and some months later, in August, 1879, the company actually constructed the first water works on the north side of the bayou near what was called "Stanley's brick yard," where they have remained ever since. The service, however, was abominable and pleased no one. The company built a dam across the bayou so as to shut off tide water and secure as pure water as possible from the upper bayou. It was totally unfit to drink and no one ever thought of using it for that purpose.

In the early nineties it was discovered that an abundant supply of the purest artesian water could be obtained anywhere in Houston, and the water works company sank several artesian wells. That gave Houston an abundant supply of pure drinking water. However, the standpipe was too small, or for some other reason the company claimed they could not supply the city with both drinking water and water for protection against fire, and every time a fire occurred they would pump bayou water into the reservoir, with the result that the water became unfit to drink for some time after every fire.

The people complained, but that did no good. Finally, in 1906, under the administration of Mayor Baldwin Rice, the city purchased the plant outright, for $901,000, and since that time there has been no complaint nor any reason for complaint. This is the only public utility owned by the city, but its record has been a good one, so much so as to create something of a general desire that the city take over some others and run them in the interest of the people as the water works are now run. As one evidence of how the people have gained by the change, it may be said that the old company was charging 50¢ per thousand gallons for water, but the city at once reduced this charge to 15¢, employed more men to add to the efficiency, and has done all this without the loss of a cent of the taxpayers' money.

After serving two terms, Mr. Wilson retired and was succeeded by Mr. A. J. Burke. There was nothing accomplished during this administration for the very good and simple reason that nothing could be accomplished. Efforts were made to compromise the huge city debt, but the bondholders stood firm and nothing could be done.

When Mr. Burke's term expired, some of the leading men of Houston conceived a great idea. They determined to apply expert business methods and nothing else in settling the city's affairs. A committee, composed of the best businessmen of the city, called on Mr. Wm. R. Baker and asked him to devote his superb financial ability towards solving the great financial problem which confronted the city. He, after some hesitation, consented to do so, but made it one of the conditions that he should name the men who were to serve as aldermen with him. This was granted and he named a number of the leading bankers, merchants and businessmen as his staff. There was no serious opposition to the ticket and it was elected by practically a unanimous vote.

When the city was turned over to those gentlemen, the bondholders became very confident. Before that they were growing uneasy, to say the least, for the people were becoming desperate and everybody was talking about throwing up the city charter and repudiating the unjust debt that had been forced on the city. However, when Houston was placed in the hands of such prominent businessmen and great financiers, doubt and fear disappeared, for the bondholders knew that these gentlemen could not afford to be mixed up in anything such as repudiating a debt. Already something like repudiation had taken place, for the citizens had held an election and decided that not more than 50¢ on the dollar should be paid for the bonds. This action tied the hands of the Baker administration, of course, and they could do nothing, for the bondholders would not accept 50¢ on the dollar.

Towards the middle of the Baker administration a final effort was made. Mr. Wm. D. Cleveland and Mr. J. Waldo, two of the aldermen, went to New York for a conference with the bondholders, who were showing an inclination to "listen to reason." After some discussion the bondholders agreed to compromise for 60¢ on the dollar and to take forty-year bonds, a new issue. The aldermen explained that the action of the citizens precluded their paying more than 50¢.

Then the bondholders made a proposition. The compromise would be made ostensibly for 60¢ on the dollar, but really for 40¢. A prominent Houston banker, Mr. Baker, and Mr. Cleveland were to guarantee that the new bonds would be issued by the city and for doing this the bondholders would divide the difference between 40¢ and 60¢ with these three men and keep quiet about it. The aldermen returned to Houston, and Mr. Cleveland, Mayor Baker and the banker went over the proposition.

Mr. Cleveland pointed out that the plan proposed offered the only solution of the problem and suggested that the three gentlemen draw up an agreement, together with a statement of facts, by which the city would get all the bonds that were, ostensibly, set aside for themselves; that this agreement be witnessed by reputable witnesses and locked up securely in a safe. The bondholders had said they would treat the matter confidentially. Mr. Cleveland and Mr. Baker saw the advantage to the city and were anxious to close the deal, but the banker was afraid and dreaded adverse criticism and discussion by the people who would know nothing of the truth of the deal until it was all over. He refused to have anything to do with it and as the bondholders insisted on his taking part, the thing fell through. Houston lost the opportunity of compromising her debt on the most advantageous conditions that were ever offered.

With so many bonds out, some of them were in weak hands. These small holders, either willingly or unwillingly, parted with their holdings for about

35 cents on the dollar. The Baker administration was enabled to pick up a great many bonds in that way, but the large holders stood firm. Buying the bonds, as Mayor Baker did, reduced the bonded debt, of course, but it was borrowing from Peter to pay Paul, for at the close of the Baker administration the floating debt of the city was about $200,000 greater than when it went in.

Having tried expert business methods and failed, the people arose in their might and went to the opposite extreme. They turned out the financiers and put Mr. D. C. Smith and what was called a "short hair" board of aldermen in office. The labor ticket was elected triumphantly, and in electing these gentlemen, the citizens did a wise thing. When the news reached New York that the city had been turned over to the labor element, there was consternation in the bondholders' camp. They could see nothing but repudiation and ruin ahead of them, and their greatest fear was that the debt might be repudiated before their agents could get here with offers of compromise. After some bickering, which served to delay action by the council if in no other way, the bondholders came to an agreement with the city by the terms of which the debt was compromised on a basis that permitted the city to make needed improvements and pay interest regularly on the reduced debt. Since that day the city has been free from great financial embarrassment.

It seems strange to say in one breath that Houston has the best and the most dangerous form of government that could possibly be conceived. And yet that is literally true. The form, as all know, gives almost absolute power to a few men chosen, not by wards as was done formerly, but by all the people of the city regardless of ward and sub-ward divisions. The advantages of this method are apparent, for the Mayor, or Chairman, and each Commissioner represents the whole city and not any particular part of it. Each is responsible to the whole people and not, as formerly, to that one part of it where he might chance to have lived and from which he was chosen by the votes of his friends and neighbors only. He owes no political debt to any single ward and it becomes his duty to legislate for the good of the city as a whole and not for any subdivision of it.

The dangerous feature is the power the commission form gives a few men. Should a dishonest or incompetent Board of Commissioners chance to secure election, the result might be disastrous before the people awoke to their peril and took steps to check it. Of course, such a condition as that is very unlikely to occur. Still there is a possibility of its occurring and in that one thing alone lies the danger. The mere fact that there is danger in the form assures its safety, for it puts the voters on their guard and they are more careful than ever they were under the old method, in selecting their servants, so that it is almost impossible for unworthy or incompetent men to be elected. If the commission had nothing else to recommend it, this placing the voters on their guard would be a sufficient endorsement of its merits.

The evolution of the Commission idea has been slow and tedious, and it is remarkable that it has taken great disasters to impress its merits upon the minds of interested communities. Following the two great yellow fever epidemics of 1878 and 1879 in Memphis, Tennessee, the people of that city found themselves bankrupt and forced to adopt the untried and desperate remedy of ceasing to be an incorporated city and instead becoming a taxing district under a commission. That was, as a matter of fact, the first time the commission idea was applied practically to the management and direction of municipal affairs. It was not until the great disaster at Galveston in September, 1900, that anything like a practical commission for the government of a city was devised. Galveston, by act of the Legislature, was granted a new charter which did away with the old mayor and board of aldermen and placed municipal affairs in the hands of five commissioners—a mayor, or chairman, a commissioner of finance, a commissioner of streets and alleys, a commissioner of water works, lights, etc., and a commissioner of police and fire departments.

These are all elected by the whole vote of the city and each commissioner is given full charge of his department and held responsible for its working. The other commissioners have the authority to overrule and veto any undesirable act of any one of their members, but this has never been necessary, for the ability and honesty of the men thus far elected by the people have been such as to render unnecessary the exercise of the veto power by the other commissioners. If argument were necessary to show the merits of the Commission form of municipal government, the success of that in Galveston would be sufficient.

The success of the Galveston Commission attracted wide attention and in 1904 the plan was submitted to the voters of Houston and, they having adopted it, the next year a new charter was granted the city, under which Houston became a Commission city. Houston's charter differs in many respects from those of Galveston, Dallas and other cities that have gone under commission rule. Its practical working is so well shown in an address delivered by Mayor Rice before the Chicago Commercial Club in December, 1910, that it may be well to take the following points from that address so as to best illustrate the commission:

> The essential differences between the old form of municipal government and the commission form are three. The substitution of a smaller number of aldermen elected from the city at large, in place of a large number of aldermen elected from different wards or subdivisions of the city; vesting of a coordinate power in the mayor as in the city council to dismiss any officer of the city government, except the controller, at any time without cause, and the essential provisions safeguarding the granting of municipal franchises. Instead of a body of twelve aldermen elected from different wards of the city, under the Houston system four aldermen are elected from the body of the city by the votes of all the citizens, in the same way in which the mayor is elected.
>
> These four aldermen, together with the mayor, constitute the city council or legislative department of the city government. The executive power is vested in the mayor, but by an ordinance, for the administration of the city's affairs, a large part of executive or administrative power is subdivided into different departments, and a committee is placed over each department, and one of the four aldermen, nominated by the mayor, is what is known as the active chairman.
>
> The mayor and all four aldermen are members of each committee. The active chairman of the committee practically has control of the administration of the department, unless his views are overruled by the whole committee, but by the organization of the committees the active chairman does the work, to a certain extent, under the supervision and direction of the mayor, who is, in the last analysis, the head of each committee and the person in whom the executive power of the municipal government ultimately rests.
>
> Under the old system of government, by which twelve aldermen were elected from as many different precincts of the city,

it frequently happened that unfit men came to represent certain wards of the city council. Now, unless a man has sufficient standing and reputation throughout the body of the city as a fit man for the office of alderman he will not be elected. Again, each alderman under the present system represents the whole city. Under the old system the conduct of public business was continually obstructed by a system of petty log-rolling going on among and between the representatives of the numerous subdivisions of the city. Then, too, the smallness of the number of aldermen now affords opportunity for the transaction of business.

An executive session is held previous to each meeting of the city council, at which matters to come before the council are discussed and action determined on. The small number of aldermen enables the city administration to act on all matters of importance as a unit. In other words, the system makes it possible to administer the affairs of the city in a prompt and businesslike way.

This is one of the strongest arguments in favor of the present commission form of government, for with a majority of the aldermen always in session, public business can be, and is, promptly attended to. It is no longer necessary to go before the city council with petitions to have something done. Any citizen who desires to have a street paved, taxes adjusted, a nuisance abated, or anything else, has only to call at the mayor's office and have the matter promptly adjusted. After a hearing, the matter is decided by the council in the presence of the applicant. To illustrate the great difference between this method and the old one, the following comparison is made:

By the old method a petition was addressed to the council. This was then referred to a committee, which acted when convenient. Then a report to the council was made by the committee. After the action of the council, it went to the mayor and from the mayor to someone else for execution. The people do not pay their taxes for such treatment. They want their business attended to promptly and that is what is being done under the commission.

This July, the commission will have been in existence seven years, and during that time it has accomplished wonders. In 1905 the floating debt of the city was about $400,000. Every cent of that has been wiped out and the taxpayers have been given, out of the treasury, without the issuance of a single bond for any one of the items, the following permanent improvements:

City Attorney, Law Library......$974.10
Assessor & Collector,
Block Book System................10,000.00
City Hall,
Furniture & Fixtures.............1,123.67
Police Department...................4,096.03
Fire Department,
Buildings & Equipment........66,239.67
Electrical Department...........37,461.47
Health Department................7,340.94
Parks....................................116,451.09
Streets & Bridges...................71,004.96
Asphalt Plant.........................,3,000.00
Auditorium...........................390,340.92
Ship Channel.......................102,536.05
Sewers..................................132,047.56
Paving Streets......................221,006.00
Water Department,
Extension of Mains &
Improvements......................325,757.33
Wharves and Slips.................33,109.89
School Buildings.................356,477.20
Total Improvements........$1,878,966.88

Extraordinary Expenses
Storrie Certificates..............$73,300.00
Refund Paving Certificates...141,418.68
Sinking Fund.....................120,220.00
$334,938.68

This makes a grand total of $2,213,905.56, all of which was paid out of current revenues, and the elimination of a floating debt amounting to a little more than $400,000. One need go no further than those figures to be convinced of the benefits and advantages of Commission form of government.

Unquestionably the magnificent form of government that Houston has, and the thoroughly businesslike manner in which the affairs of the city are administered, have had helped in establishing confidence in the stability of the city both at home and abroad. Though the commission may not have caused it, the fact remains that coincident with the establishment of the commission Houston began to grow and expand in the most marvelous way. Strangers who come here and find a large and beautiful city are amazed to learn that modern Houston is only about seven years old. All the great strides forward, all the large corporations, all the great business enterprises, are less than ten years old, while the city has more than doubled her population in seven years.

Houston is today a city of skyscrapers and large buildings, and their number is being added to monthly. There are today a number of new ones going up and nearly every principal street in the city is the scene of building activity. There are hotels completed and being constructed, office buildings, business buildings, bank buildings, to say nothing of the hundreds of residences being constructed. Houston stands in a class of its own when it comes to apartment houses, for there are more and finer ones here than in any other Texas city. They are nearly all strictly up-to-date and several of them are luxurious and costly affairs.

Just what Houston is doing today and how it is being done is well shown in the reports made by the mayor and the commissioners and heads of departments at the close of the fiscal year, February 29, 1912. Mayor Rice says:

> *Gentlemen-* According to the law, I submit the annual report of the various departments and the budget for the ensuing year.
>
> You will notice that the appropriations recommended and the budget called for is some $200,000 in excess of last year, one half alone being increase of the interest and sinking funds on bonds and additional school appropriations.
>
> The rapid growth of the city and its numerous requirements means that the growth if yearly maintained, as it has for the past

several years, the city of Houston must expend annually more revenue to maintain in efficiency the various departments and satisfy local conditions.

I shall briefly discuss the important demands of the city and make recommendations for their improvements and needs.

The water department is in splendid condition and with the extension of mains this year will probably place every one within the limits of the city of Houston in easy access of pure water and charging the lowest rate for consumption.

Houston has an efficient and up-to-date fire department, and but for the unfortunate fire which occurred in the manufacturing district on the north side of the city during a tremendous gale, would have probably maintained the smallest loss in any one year since Houston's growth. I call attention to this great conflagration from a commercial standpoint, as the great losses from the immense quantities of cotton and manufactories destroyed ran into large sums of money. While numerous small homes were destroyed, yet, I am glad to state, the majority of those thus afflicted asked for no assistance and are making plans to reconstruct their homes upon a better and safer basis.

For those who were left destitute, too much praise cannot be given to the United Charities and the kind citizens who came forward and cheerfully made subscriptions for relief. Knowing the character of people who make up this community, and feeling confident of their generosity and grit, I, as mayor, declined all outside help and subsequent events justified my position. While deeply grateful for all offers of aid from all parts of the country, Houston demonstrated that her people can and will take care of almost any calamity that may overtake them. I recommend that an appropriation of $25,000 be made for a new fire station and equipment at Westmoreland station, as suggested by Fire Commissioner Kohlhauff.

I call your attention to the annual report of streets and bridges. It demonstrates what an immense amount of work and expense it requires to drain and make passable the streets in a level country like ours. A great viaduct connecting the north and south sides of the city is now under good headway and promises when completed to be one of the most substantial structures in the State, as well as giving rapid transportation for the people. Nearly all the bridges over Buffalo Bayou are out of date and fail to properly accommodate the traffic. I recommend that the bridges at San Jacinto and Preston Streets be removed and that more substantial bridges be constructed out of reinforced concrete. I also recommend that a reinforced concrete bridge be built over Buffalo Bayou at the foot of Texas Avenue, which will relieve congestion of traffic on both Washington and Preston avenues. Houston Avenue viaduct, now being constructed, will give immense relief to that section of the city.

During the past year $500,000 of bonds were voted for school purposes, and several schoolhouses will be constructed during the fiscal year, which will give the additional facilities that are so badly needed in our growing city.

Both the school board and city commissioners have for some time been acquiring additional property for school sites and playgrounds for the children. I believe in the near future, Houston's schools and playgrounds will be a model for any city to copy.

As we have no swimming pools for boys or girls in this community, upon the recommendation of Mrs. James A. Baker, president of the Settlement Association, who is taking a deep interest in their welfare, I suggest that a natatorium be constructed on the new Rusk school site, and that the feature be gradually extended to every other school in this city. I think Superintendent Horn's recommendation, that all public schools should be used as social centers, be adopted. These school grounds and buildings cost the taxpayer a great deal of money and should be utilized in various ways. School children are dismissed daily at 3 p. m. and there is no reason after that time why the immediate neighborhood should not use the building for any social custom they desire without going to the expense of renting halls. By such gatherings in a public building, that they have helped to construct, the people will not only become better acquainted, but better satisfied with taxation.

Houston should no longer wait for a park system. Land is becoming dearer every year. While the city has purchased additional park ground during the year, yet we are very deficient in this respect. We have a splendid board of park commissioners and I recommend that the city of Houston issue at least $250,000 in park bonds or more this year in order to secure a good start.

Now that the auditorium is completed I recommend that it be used for the best interest of the community. I am very anxious to see the social conditions of our people improved, especially on Sundays. On the first of May next Houston will have one of the finest bands in the United States. It will be maintained by the city. Not only will there be instrumental music, but some of the best vocal music in the country.

In addition to the musical part of the afternoons' and nights' entertainments on Sunday there can be secured good, wholesome picture shows, lectures and other entertainments that will tend to educate the people and make them happy and contented. All these entertainments will be free for the people and especially to the working classes will this program be satisfactory, as they can enjoy the best music and best lectures at absolutely no cost. Once inaugurated and well established, I believe this work of our city government will go a long way toward exterminating some of the vicious tendencies that trouble our cities.

This government, in fulfilling its promises, created a public service department last year, and appointed a commissioner for that purpose. I recommend that every citizen read Mr. Gaston's report and know what has been accomplished.

I am glad to state that the efficiency of the police department is gradually being raised, and I trust in the near future that it will be up to the standard.

During the present year the Somers system of taxation has been established in Houston, at the suggestion of Commissioner Pastoriza. It seems to be a very efficient system, just and equitable to all. The tax board has adopted the system of assessing land values at 90 per cent and improvements at 25 per cent of their value. Under this system the valuations have been increased from $77,000,000 to $123,000,000, which is very great. All tax problems are difficult, and very few, if any, are satisfactory. I would suggest that the citizens thoroughly investigate this system and understand it. If it is satisfactory, so much the better; if not, then some better plan should be proposed. The city council will not be arbitrary, but will be glad to listen to any one or all citizens upon this subject. Last year the tax rate was $1.70 per $100. This year it has been reduced to $1.30 per hundred for all purposes, being the lowest rate of any large city in the State.

With the exception of a few cases of meningitis...the health of this community has been splendid. Too much praise cannot be given our health officer, Dr. G. W. Larendon, and specialist, Dr. F. J. Slataper, and their associates for the way the health department has been managed. On account of the amount of work and the risks that these gentlemen are required to run I am decidedly in favor of increasing their respective salaries.

Now that the national government will soon commence work upon our waterway, I suggest that the city acquire more territory at the turning basin. I suggest steps be taken to condemn all land that is needed for practical purposes, and also that the city of Houston build and maintain a modern dredge boat on the channel.

The city has recently adopted a front-foot plan of pavement. It is a great step forward in progress and means that Houston will now go forward with rapid strides. Already petitions have been placed with the council for over ten miles of pavement. I caution the people that no permanent pavement should be made until all water, gas and sewer mains are first laid. I earnestly recommend that a million dollars be issued in bonds for sanitary and storm sewers alone. A short-time paving bond can be issued, redeemable at the rate of, say, $200,000 per year, which will give immediate relief in regard to the pavements and not increase the bonded indebtedness.

The city needs a city jail and additional fireproof rooms to the city hall to preserve city records. I recommend that an annex to the city hall be constructed to care for all these various features.

Thanking you for your hearty cooperation, I am,

Respectfully,

H. B. Rice

An idea of what it costs to run a big city like Houston may be formed from the following recommendations, made by the mayor, for the coming year:

Mayor and Commissioners	$13,600
Controller and Secretary	7,500
Law Department	12,000
Treasurer	620
Assessor & Collector	18,000
City Hall	4,000
Elections	1,000
Damages	1,000
Interest on bonds	265,000
Sinking fund	140,000
Miscellaneous expenses	15,000
Electric lights	50,000
Police	110,000
Corporation court	2,500
Fire department	125,000
Health department	25,000
Scavenger department	13,000
Electrical department	8,000
City engineer	20,000
Streets and bridges	100,000
Repair of shell & gravel streets	25,000
Sewer department	25,000
Garbage department	25,000
Market	7,000
Schools	210,000
Parks	10,000
Carnegie library	10,000
Refunding certificates	21,000
Buffalo Bayou	5,000
Mayor's emergency fund	1,000
Westmoreland fire station & equipment	25,000
Water department (general)	80,000
Interest	55,000
Sinking fund	28,000
Total	$1,458,220

Perhaps more interest attaches to the report of City Tax Commissioner Pastoriza this year than to any of the others, because of some radical changes that have been made in methods of taxation during the year just closed.

He states in his report that in the beginning of 1911 city officials were confronted with the necessity of raising the assessment over $12,000,000 to produce the additional revenue needed. He says that while the work for 1911 was fairly well done, the experience gained has convinced him of the necessity of a scientific plan of assessment. The Somers system largely solved the problem with its system of equalizing the value by a mathematical rule for calculation. A contract was entered into with the Manufacturers' Appraisal Company of Cleveland to install the system and for the past four months that work has been in progress. In his report Commissioner Pastoriza says:

> The application of the Somers system has revealed the fact that portions of many streets of Houston, some of them of exceeding value, are being used by individual citizens and corporations without bringing the city any rental or compensation whatever, and I recommend therefore that I be given authority to immediately institute suits to recover this valuable property for the city and to have removed such buildings or other obstructions as now occupy them.
>
> I also discovered that the area of many pieces of land were not accurately stated upon the block maps. There was not sufficient time to enable me to have these lands surveyed for the 1912 assessment, and I ask to be given authority to have these lands surveyed and that the engineering department be instructed to place at my disposal such help as is necessary to do this work without interruption and with the least delay possible.

The report shows that the tax rate was reduced from $1.70 in 1910 to $1.30 on the $100 in 1911. Commissioner Pastoriza explains in his report:

> To the average mind this might indicate a reduction in the rate of taxation, but Houston is a growing city, growing at a rate which few people realize, and the ever increasing need for street paving, drainage, sewers, extension of water mains, schools and playgrounds, for police and fire protection and a hundred and

one improvements not enumerated, calls for an ever increasing revenue.

In conclusion permit me to say that we do not claim our values are absolutely correct, but we do claim that they have been equalized as nearly as is possible, and that if our valuation of any particular piece of property in a block is considered too high, at least everybody else in that block and in the block across the street will be equally high; if we are low, everybody in that block and across the street will be equally low and there will be no discrimination. We have learned that it is not so much a question in the mind of a taxpayer whether our values are too high or too low, so long as we assess everybody the same, and only make the rate high enough to give the administration sufficient money to economically administer its affairs.

The report compiled by Building Inspector W. X. Norris shows that during the last fiscal year of the city permits were issued out of his office for the construction of 110 buildings of all kinds at an aggregate cost of $3,997,000. The permits issued during the previous fiscal year reached an aggregate of $3,152,820. Besides the permanent improvements permits were also issued last year for temporary work, aggregating $281,375, as against temporary work amounting to $189,270 during the previous year.

In his report the building inspector recommends that the electric sign ordinance be revised so as to provide for all electric signs to be hung vertical with the building. The permits issued by the building inspector have been classified by him in the following manner:

Permits	Kind of Building	# of Bldgs	Valuation
1	18-story fireproof hotel	1	$500,000
1	10-story fireproof hotel	1	$195,000
1	7-story fireproof office bldg	1	$150,000
1	6-story fireproof hotel	1	$70,000
1	6-story fireproof office bldg	1	$135,000
1	4-story fireproof bldg	1	$150,000
2	3-story fireproof bldgs	2	$117,000
1	3-story brick hotel & theatre bldg	1	$65,000
2	3-story brick flats	2	$31,300
4	3-story brick bldgs	4	$126,500

Permits	Kind of Building	# of Bldgs	Valuation
1	3-story brick warehouse	1	$4,500
1	3-story brick office bldg	1	$14,000
1	3-story concrete bldg & remodeling	1	$60,000
5	2-story brick warehouses	5	$61,000
2	2-story brick flats	2	$32,000
2	2-story brick stores	2	$9,000
1	2-story brick office bldg	1	$33,000
5	2-story brick bldgs	51	$36,300
3	2-story brick residences	3	$87,500
1	2-story concrete bldg	1	$40,000
1	2-story concrete warehouse	1	$14,000
3	2-story frame apartments	2	$22,000
1	4-story fireproof bldg	1	$150,000
5	2-story wood warehouses	5	$59,350
1	2-story stucco residence	1	$16,000
247	2-story frame residences	262	$811,985
1	Brick church	1	$56,000
6	1-story brick bldgs	6	$37,100
1	1-story brick office & car shed	1	$20,000
2	1-story brick warehouses	2	$12,000
2	1-story brick bldgs (not built)	1	$8,000
1	1-story cement block bldg	1	$3,000
3	Frame churches	3	$4,650
1	Frame clubhouse	1	$2,500
589	Cottages	748	$576,235
18	Iron & frame farehouses	19	$34,040
1	Open air theatre	1	$4,000
1	Automobile garage	1	$500
1	Fireproof addition	1	$14,900
1	Storage oil tank	1	$5,000
1	Oil plant	1	$10,650
1	Bread plant	1	$16,500
1	Viaduct	1	$350,000
2	Remodeling	2	$47,500
926		1101	$3,997,010

Valuation of 926 permits, year ending Feb. 29, 1912.........$3,997,010
Valuation of 868 permits, year ending Feb. 28, 1911.........$3,152,810

Increase in value, year ending Feb. 29, 1912........................$844,190

Valuation temporary permits, year ending Feb. 1912...........$281,375
Valuation temporary permits, year ending Feb. 1911...........$189,270

Increase for year ending Feb. 29, 1912 over 1911...................$92,105

Total value temporary & permanent for year 1912.............$4,278,385
Total value temporary & permanent for year 1912.............$3,342,090

Increase in last 12 months over previous 12 months.............$936,295

The following is a list of Houston's Mayors. The list is the one prepared by Major Roberts, though, for reasons given in the foregoing, Mr. Holman is not placed at the head:

1838	Dr. Francis Moore, Jr.
1839	G. W. Lively
1840	Charles Biglow
1841-42	J. D. Andrews
1843	Dr. Francis Moore, Jr.
1844	Horace Baldwin
1845	W. W. Swain
1846	Jas. Bailey
1847-48	P. B. Buckner
1849-52	Dr. Francis Moore, Jr.
1853-54	Col. Nathan Fuller
1855-56	Jas. H. Stevens
1857	Cornelius Ennis
1858	A. McGowan
1859	W. H. King
1860	T. W. Whitmarsh
1861	W. J. Hutchins
1862	T. W. House
1863-65	William Andrews

1866	H. D. Taylor
1867	A. McGowan
1868	J. R. Morris
1870-73	T. J. Scanlan
1874	J. T. D. Wilson
1875-76	I. C. Lord
1877-78	J. T. D. Wilson
1879	A. J. Burke
1880-84	W. R. Baker
1886-88	D. C. Smith
1890	Henry Scherrfius
1892-94	John T. Browne
1896	H. Baldwin Rice
1898-1900	Sam H. Brashear
1902	O. T. Holt
1904	Andrew L. Jackson
1905-12	H. Baldwin Rice

CHAPTER II:
GREAT MEN, GRAND STRUCTURES

When one reads the names of the early Houstonians, it is almost like reading an early joint directory of Houston and Galveston for, in the forties, many of the men who aided in establishing Houston were also instrumental in building up Galveston and their names became inseparable from the history of the two places. General E. B. Nichols was, after the fifties, one of the most progressive citizens of Galveston, but to that time he was one of the pioneer workers in Houston. In the case of Mr. B. A. Shepherd, conditions were reversed. He was first a citizen of Galveston and then of Houston. Gail Borden, who surveyed the city of Houston and made the first map of the new city, was for years a resident of Houston and then removed to Galveston, where he became one of the most enthusiastic citizens there and prophesied most of the great things that have been accomplished by that city.

The first frame house in Houston was a small affair erected by the Torrey brothers who used it as a trading post for Indians. It was located on the north side of Preston near what is now the east end of Preston street bridge. It was afterwards purchased by Mr. H. D. Taylor and used by him as a residence for many years. It was one of the most beautiful and attractive places in Houston, in the midst of a grove of magnificent magnolia trees.

On the south side of Preston and on the east side of Smith there was a single room board house, erected about the same time as the Indian trading post. This was purchased by Col. N. Fuller, in 1837, and he added other rooms to it and built the residence which he occupied until the day of his death. That and the residence erected by Mr. A. C. Briscoe on Main and Prairie were unquestionably the first two-story houses erected in Houston, and both were built in 1837, the year after the founding of Houston. An item of interest is that when the Fuller residence was torn down a year or two ago to make place for the great brick building that now occupies its site. The old and original beams and rafters were found to be in perfect preservation and resembled steel beams more than wooden ones. It was with difficulty that they were torn apart, showing how thorough and honest were the early Houston builders.

The year 1837 also witnessed the erection of the first large warehouse in Houston. This was located on the northeast corner of Main and Commerce

Streets and was built by Mr. Thomas Elsberry. It was in this building that Messrs. Allen and Pool did business for many years, and it was there also that some of the great financiers of Houston had their early training. Mr. Doswell and Mr. Wm. R. Baker had their first experience as businessmen there, and others of less prominence worked for Allen and Pool from time to time.

All the early cotton crops of Texas passed through that old building, for it was the only cotton warehouse here and its location was ideal for conditions as they prevailed then. The building fronted on Commerce Street and extended back to the crude wharf of that day. The bales were simply tumbled out of the back door and landed near the steamboat, on which they were rolled by negro deck hands. Transportation by water was the only way to reach the markets of the world, and the bayou was of far more practical importance then than it has since become.

While the carpenters were erecting the Allen and Pool warehouse, workmen were busily engaged in hewing logs for the building of Houston's first hotel, which was erected on the corner of Franklin and Travis, where the Southern Pacific offices now stand.

It was built by Major Ben Fort Smith, one of the Texas pioneers, and its first proprietor was Mr. George Wilson, father of Mr. Ed Wilson, who is still an honored citizen of Houston. This old house stood for nearly twenty years and then, in 1855, it fell down through old age and decay. In the *Houston Telegraph* of May 16, 1855, is an interesting account of its fall, and still more interesting reminiscences connected with the old building.

> It had been in its day the hotel par excellence of the Capitol and commercial metropolis of the glorious old Republic of Texas. The President and his cabinet and the senators and representatives and officials of the first and second Congresses had dined there and so, too, had foreign ministers.
>
> Rusk, who was a great man before the Republic, was once glorified at its tables with a sacrifice of good things—fowls at $6 a pair, butter at $1 per pound, eggs at $3 per dozen and champagne at a fabulous price per bottle. It has been said that the dinner was planned to encourage a reconciliation between Rusk and Houston, and that it was so far successful that Rusk, in toasting Houston, his old opponent, said: "Houston, with all thy faults I love thee still."

Texas had great men in those days and their name was legion. It was an insult to take a man for anything but great, brave, chivalrous and even rich. Everybody was rich, or in the army or navy or public service, which was the same thing. The City Hotel had a barroom, one of perhaps twenty that flourished in the town, where steam was kept up at the explosion point, and the collapse of a decanter, pitcher or tumbler, as it came in contact with the brains of some unlucky devotee of the shrine of chivalry or bravado, or the kindred virtues usually worshipped "when the wine was red in the cup," was no uncommon occurrence.

Those were the days of duels, bowie knives and pistols, poker, keno and faro, when ten, twenty or fifty thousand dollars would be lost and won in a night. Texas was the prophecy of California and Houston a very San Francisco. No mines were dug, but gold was plenty and men managed to live without sweating their brows. If a man worked at all he earned from $8 to $10 a day, but precious few worked at all.

Buck Peters and Jeff Wright were the practical jokers then. Judge Shelby was on the bench and was indicted by his own grand jury for playing backgammon with his wife. Gus Tompkins, fertile in expedient but fractious, with his big brain and little body, was a terror to evildoers. Felix Huston commanded the turbulent army. Commodore Moore had not come to Texas then, and the navy was divided with several competent but less ambitious commanders, not less distinguished among them was our old friend Boots Taylor, a very Chesterfield in manners. Carnes and Teel and Morehouse and Deaf Smith lived in those times with a host of other noble spirits whose lights have long since gone out.

We notice a few survivors of those glorious days still among us. Col. Frank Johnson, one of the heroes of the storming of San Antonio, and the surrender of the Mexican garrison under Cos, sat with us on a log under the very eaves of the old building the day before it fell, and with him another survivor, Honest Bob Wilson, who was expelled from the Senate of the old Republic, but was re-elected and borne back in triumph upon the shoulders of an indignant people to the Capitol.

During 1837-39 there were a great number of houses erected in Houston, but all were wooden structures or primitive log cabins. Not until nine years after the town was established was a brick building put up. In 1845 Mr. Cornelius Ennis and General E. B. Nichols erected two brick buildings on the east side of Main Street, between Congress and Commerce Avenues. One was where the Western Union Telegraph Office now is and the other was where the Converse building is located.

Seven years later, in 1852, Mr. Paul Bremond erected a brick building and the following year Mr. B. A. Shepherd erected his bank building on the corner of Main and Congress, across the street from the present magnificent Union Bank building. All these first brick buildings were small two-story affairs, and as small as they were they seem to have been ahead of the time for in most of them the second stories were used only as lumber rooms.

On March 10, 1859, the first note of Houston's real progress was sounded by the fire bell. At the time it was regarded as a great disaster, and from a money point of view it was something of the kind, since the loss was placed at about $300,000, with little or no insurance. A great fire broke out at midnight on the corner of Main and Congress, and raged for eight hours. All the block on the west side of Main between Preston and Congress was destroyed and half of the block on the opposite side of Main was also consumed. These houses were wooden shanties and their destruction was the best thing that could have happened.

Almost before the ground grew cold again workmen were busy digging trenches for foundations, and in a short time several really fine brick buildings were erected. Mr. Wm. Van Alstyne, father of Mr. A. A. Van Alstyne, now of Galveston, had the honor of erecting the first three-story building in Houston. It was a very attractive building and stood on the corner of Main and Congress, directly opposite the present Krupp and Tuffly building. But Mr. J. R. Morris outdid Mr. Van Alstyne, for he put up a four-story iron-front building, not only the first of its kind in Houston, but the first ever erected in Texas. The building was in the middle of the block on the east side of Main, between Preston and Congress Avenues.

It was not a fire, or disaster of any kind, that gave Houston its first great hotel. During the same year that the Van Alstyne and Morris buildings were erected, Col. Wm. J. Hutchins began the erection of a large four-story hotel built of brick on the historic site of Houston's first hotel. This was the famous Hutchins House, made famous by the fact that most of the State associations, societies and many of the large commercial enterprises had their inception in its parlors.

To that time and ever since 1837, when the State Capitol building was erected, which was later the Old Capitol Hotel, it had been Houston's chief hotel. This was a rather commodious frame building, two-stories in height, and stood on the site where the new 18-story Rice Hotel is now being erected, corner of Main and Texas avenue. The Hutchins House was not completed until after the war; that is, not completely so, and there was a long delay before it could be used for the purpose for which it was designed. This historic house was burned down several years ago and the ground was allowed to remain vacant until 1911 when it was purchased by the Southern Pacific Railroad and the present magnificent office building of that road was erected on it.

In 1859 and 1860 Houston had something of a building boom and a great many really pretentious (for that day) buildings were erected in various parts of the city. One or two rather extensive fires occurred about that time, which cleared the ground of wooden shacks and enabled the owners to build more substantial houses, which they did.

For some years after the war there was very little in the way of improvements. During the war it was impossible to do much and after peace had been declared the people were too poor to do anything that was not absolutely imperative. The skyline of Houston underwent no changes until 1894, when Jacob Binz erected the first skyscraper in Houston. This building is still standing and though there are many others that tower high above it, it is justly considered one of the most useful and substantial buildings of its class in Houston. This building occupies one of the historic sites of the city, for it stands where the first Land Office of the Republic was situated, when Houston was the capital of Texas. Its erection marked the beginning of a new era for Houston architecturally. It was the introduction of the modern skyscraper, buildings for which Houston has since grown famous. Today Houston has more skyscrapers than any city in Texas and many more are planned.

The first public buildings in Houston were the County courthouse and the County jail, erected in 1838 by Harrisburg County, as Harris County was then called. They were both primitive in every sense of the word. The courthouse was a double log cabin, with a broad passage between the two rooms, such a building as is still occasionally seen on old plantations. The rooms were each sixteen feet square, the court being in one room and the clerk's office in the other. The jail was something of a curiosity, being simply a square log box with neither doors nor windows. There was but one opening, that being a trapdoor at the top. Access to the jail was through this trapdoor. A prisoner was taken to the roof by means of a ladder. The ladder was then drawn up and lowered into the jail. The prisoner descended and then the ladder was drawn up and the trap shut. It was all very simple, but very cumbersome as well.

Both the jail and courthouse were located on the Congress Avenue side of Courthouse Square, near Fannin. They answered very well for the court needs of that day, but the city and county soon outgrew them and it became necessary to provide better and more commodious quarters. Since the city had constructed the old market house and provided quite a serviceable city lock-up, or calaboose, the county solved the jail problem by making a contract with the city whereby the county was allowed to make use of the city prison as a county jail. The old log courthouse was still used, however, until 1850, when it was torn down and the first brick courthouse was erected. The building was placed almost in the center of the block, but a little to the Congress side. It was a two-story brick building, cost $15,000, and was regarded as the finest building in the country by the early Houstonians.

Owing to poor material, faulty construction or some other cause, this first courthouse did not stand long. Its walls cracked so badly and it showed such evidence of decay that nine years after its erection it was condemned and torn down to make way for a second brick building.

The second brick courthouse was erected in 1859. This was a much larger and more expensive building than its predecessor. It was placed on the north side of the square, fronting Congress Avenue. It was really a three-story building for it had a large basement, which was used for offices by some of the county officials. The other county officials were located on the second floor, while the third floor was used entirely for court purposes, there being two large courtrooms. During the war the basement was fixed up for a guardhouse, iron bars were placed in the windows and doors and, at various times, prisoners of war, captured at Galveston and Sabine Pass were confined there. It was not used permanently for that purpose, however.

Ten years after it was built, this building also began to crumble and in 1869 it was torn down and another larger building was erected almost on

the same site, only a little further back from Congress Avenue. This courthouse was an improvement over those that had preceded it and was also
more substantially constructed, for it stood thirteen years. In 1882 it was
somewhat damaged by a windstorm, and, since it was rather dilapidated in
every way, the County Commissioners decided to tear it down and erect a
new and finer building.

There was a great deal of friction between the members of the court over
plans and financial matters, but finally everything was amicably settled and
the courthouse was built in 1883. The new building was much more pretentious than any of the others that had preceded it and it was evidently better
constructed for it served the purpose for which it had been constructed
for nearly a quarter of a century, from 1883 until 1907. In 1907, a special
election was held and an issue of $500,000 of bonds was authorized for the
purpose of building a courthouse in every way worthy of the great County
of Harris and the great City of Houston. The bonds were issued and the
present magnificent courthouse was erected. It is one of the finest buildings of its kind in the South and would be a credit to a city fives times the
population of Houston.

Mr. O. L. Cochran, who has the distinction of being the oldest citizen
of Houston, and who for many years was the postmaster here, furnishes
the following information about the early locations of the Houston Post
Office:

During the days of the Texas Republic it was located on the west
side of Main Street, about the middle of the block between Preston and Congress Avenues. After Texas became a State of the
Union, in 1845, the office was removed to the old hotel, corner
of Franklin Avenue and Travis Street. It was then removed to Dr.
Hull's drug store, corner of Preston and Main, the site of the present Fox building. Then it was removed to Courthouse Square and
located on the northeast corner of Congress Avenue and Fannin
Street. It remained here for many years and then was removed just
across the street to the northwest corner of Congress and Fannin.
The next move was to the rear of the Fox building on the north
side of Preston. Then it was taken to the Miller building on the
northwest corner of Fannin and Preston. Its stay here was not long
and its next move was to the Taylor building on the southwest cor-

ner of Preston and San Jacinto. It remained in the Taylor building until 1890, when the government purchased the southeast corner of Franklin and Fannin and erected its own building there. That building was behind the times and Houston grew so rapidly that by the time it was completed, substations had to be established to handle the business.

In 1903 the Government purchased the block in front of the High School and erected on it the present fine building, completed only a few months ago. Although the building is very large and thoroughly equipped, Houston has again outgrown it, and it has been found necessary to retain the old building, which is to be remodeled, improved and used as a substation.

As told elsewhere, Houston's first market house was erected in 1840 and stood until 1871, when it was torn down to make place for the great brick market erected at such immense cost to the taxpayers by the scalawag Reconstruction city administration. This famous building was destroyed by fire in 1876 and a similar structure was built on the same site, though for significantly less cost. In fact, the new building cost only about $80,000 to build, while the old one cost $470,000. This new building was also destroyed by fire in 1901, and then the present magnificent market house and city hall combined was erected. Today there is to be found no equal so far as usefulness, beauty of architecture and honest construction in the entire South.

It is a singular fact that Houston formerly had a volunteer fire company that was older than the city itself; that is, older than the chartered city. This was Protection No. 1, which was organized in 1836. It was not only Houston's first fire company, but it was unquestionably the first fire company organized in Texas. Houston at that time was only an aggregation of tents and log shanties, so there was no great danger of big conflagrations, and fighting fire was not the serious thing it became after more pretentious buildings were erected. Still there was danger and the company was organized to meet that danger.

For the first fourteen or fifteen years of the company's existence the method and appliances for fighting fire were extremely crude, consisting only of the formation of a line of men and the passing of buckets filled with water. The company was merely a bucket brigade, but it did good work. About 1850 the company purchased its first engine, which was a hand engine, worked by beams on each side. This old engine was used for many years and figured prominently at all the early fires, including the two or three great ones that occurred in the late fifties. It is regrettable that the names of these early Houston firemen have not been preserved.

Protection No. 1 was Houston's only fire company from 1836 until 1858. Since the city had grown and since a great fire had occurred in 1858, it became evident that better protection against fire was an imperative necessity. Hook and Ladder Company No. 1 was organized in 1858 and two years later, in 1860, Liberty No. 2 was organized. Then the great war came on and it was not until between 1866 and 1870 that further additions to the department were made. During the latter part of the war the engines were handled by negroes under control of white officers.

Mr. T. W. House, Sr., who was Mayor of the city in 1862, organized the first Houston Fire Department. The Department was composed of Protection No. 1, Hook and Ladder No. 2, and Liberty No. 2. Mr. E. L. Bremond was made Chief of the Department, and H. F. Hurd and Robert Burns were appointed First and Second Chiefs. The Department was not a great success and did not last long. There was friction between the companies and so each one pulled out and acted independently and the Department died a natural death.

It was not until 1874 that another attempt was made to organize a Department. That year Mr. J. H. B. House, son of the organizer of the first Department, succeeded in getting all the companies in the city to consent to the organization and he formed a really strong and efficient Department. Mr. J. H. B. House was unanimously elected Chief, and Messrs. Z. T. Hogan and C. C. Beavens were elected 1st and 2nd Assistants, as named. Mr. House and Mr. Hogan resigned before the end of their first term, and Mr. W. Williams was elected Chief, C. C. Beavens, First Assistant Chief, and Fred Harvey, Second Assistant.

The following is a synopsis of the report of the celebration of San Jacinto Day, as well as information about the participation of the companies in the day's festivities, as taken from the files of the *Houston Telegraph* of April 22, 1875.

There was a great street parade in which were large delegations from several interior cities, mostly from points on the Houston & Texas Central railroad. Col. J. P. Likens delivered an address during the afternoon. The following local companies were in line:

Protection No. 1—Charles Wichman, foreman; L. Ollre, first assistant; S. M. McAshan, president; Robert Brewster, secretary; R. Cohen, treasurer.

Hook and Ladder, No. 1—H. P. Roberts, president; L. Blanton, vice-president; William Cameron, secretary; O. L. Cochran, treasurer; Dr. Thorn. Robinson, foreman; J. C. Hart, first assistant; G. W. Gazley, second assistant.

Stonewall, No. 3—Joseph F. Meyer, foreman; L. M. Jones, first assistant; F. J. Frank, second assistant; W. Long, president; F. Ludke, vice-president; W. E. Smith, secretary.

Brooks, No. 5—I. C. Ford, foreman; William Alexander, first assistant; J. C. Thomas, Jr., second assistant; J. C. Thomas, Sr., president; I. Snowball, vice-president; S. L. Mateer, secretary; Thos. Milner, treasurer.

Eagle, No. 7—John Shearn, Jr., foreman; Willie Van Alstyne, first assistant; Ed. Mather, second assistant.

The *Telegraph* added the following bit of information about the companies taking part in the parade:

> Protection No. 1, organized in 1836.
> Houston Hook and Ladder No. 1, organized April 17, 1858
> Liberty No. 2, organized 1860.
> Stonewall No. 3, organized in the late sixties.
> Brooks No. 5, organized in the late sixties.
> Mechanic No. 6, organized October 28, 1873.
> Eagle No. 7, organized in 1875.

At that time the Department had two steamers, one extinguisher engine, two hand wagons and one hook and ladder company. It cost about $9,000 annually to run the department.

The old volunteer department existed as a whole for nineteen years, then, in 1893, it became a part pay and a part volunteer department. That proved unsatisfactory and the city took over the whole department in 1895, with the result that Houston has, today, one of the most useful and efficient fire departments in the South. There are thirty pieces of fire-fighting apparatus, of which nine are powerful modern steamers. In 1875 it cost $9,000 annually to run the department. Today it costs very nearly $125,000.

For some years after Houston was founded there was little or no necessity for crossing to the north side of the bayou. Very few people lived on that side and these came and went on small foot bridges which answered very well for the requirements of the limited travel. It is true that there was a growing wagon trade with other parts of the State and Houston but this was easily accommodated. All the trade from the west and northwest came in over the San Felipe road. That from the north came into the city by Stockbridge's ford, which was situated at the foot of Texas Avenue, while trade from the San Jacinto and Trinity came by the way of the Harrisburg ferry. The old San Felipe road remained unchanged to the end, but the trade from other parts of the State soon grew to such large proportions that the primitive methods of ford and ferry had to be abandoned and, in 1843, the first bridge over Buffalo Bayou was built at the foot of Preston Avenue.

That bridge stood for ten years, but was swept away by a great flood which occurred in 1853. The bridge that was constructed in its place had remarkable height and length. Its builders determined that it should not share the fate of its predecessor, so they built its center very high and extended its ends high up on each bank of the bayou. It was appropriately named "Long Bridge," and though seriously threatened by high water on several occasions it always escaped destruction. Finally, in the great flood of 1878, it was so badly damaged that it became necessary to remodel it and the present Preston Street bridge is the result. At about the same time that the Preston bridge was built a bridge was built across the bayou at the foot of Milam Street and another across White Oak bayou at the same point the present White Oak bridge occupies.

These bridges were originally cheap wooden structures, but were remodeled and ironwork substituted for wood, except in the White Oak bridge. It is utterly impossible to estimate the value of goods and produce that have passed over these bridges. For years everything grown in Texas for the outside markets was brought to Houston over them, while all goods and groceries shipped to the interior went out by the same routes. In time the Preston bridge became of chief importance, because the section north of Houston became more rapidly developed and the trade was consequently immense in that direction.

Of course when the railroads were built, the bridges were no longer needed for the purpose for which they were originally built. By that time, however, the city had grown and extended so that the bridges became equally as necessary for intercommunication between the various sections of the city as they had been for communication with the interior of the State. More bridges became necessary and more were constructed until now there are half a dozen passenger bridges and numerous railroad bridges spanning Buffalo Bayou, while an immense bridge is being constructed at the foot of Main street so as to connect with the Fifth Ward.

CHAPTER III:
BY RAIL AND BAYOU

Ask ten men and the chances are that nine of them will say that the first railroad ever built in Texas had its start in Houston. This is no doubt due to the fact that the first road that ever amounted to anything, in the early days, the Houston & Texas Central, actually did have its beginning here. As a matter of fact, railroad building began (though nothing was accomplished) thirteen years before work on the Houston & Texas Central commenced. The mistake is quite natural for Houston has been the starting point for so many of the things that have made Texas great that it seems safe to credit her with being the mother of them all.

The first railroad construction ever done in Texas, if grading a few miles of track may be called construction, was at Harrisburg in 1840. Mr. A. Brisco was the moving spirit in that enterprise and he formed a company, putting up as a bonus a number of lots in the City of Harrisburg. The company he formed had no charter nor did they try to get one. Their idea was to build the road from Harrisburg to the Brazos and, after they had earned enough money by the traffic from that rich section to justify it, extend it further west towards Gonzales.

A large force of negroes was put to work grading the roadbed and nearly two miles were completed and ties purchased for that length of road when it was found that the cost of the iron rails would be too great, so the undertaking was abandoned. The next year, however, they took out a charter under the name of the Harrisburg Railroad & Trading Company. Though they had a charter now, they made no further attempt to actually construct the road. Everything was allowed to lie dormant until 1847 when General Sidney Sherman associated himself with a number of prominent Houston and Galveston men, secured the lots offered by Mr. Brisco, and after being assured of financial support by New York capitalists, he reorganized the road and secured another charter for it under the name Buffalo Bayou, Brazos & Colorado Railroad. That road afterwards became the Galveston, Harrisburg & San Antonio railroad of today.

Though General Sherman and his associates organized in 1847, it was not until 1851 that actual work was commenced. The preparation of the roadbed was commenced and pushed as rapidly as possible, but it was a year before rails were laid. That part of the work was done rapidly, however, and before the close of the year the road was actually completed as far as the Brazos, 32 miles from Harrisburg. No stop was made, but the road was pushed forward and in 1860, Alleyton, 79 miles from Harrisburg, was reached. Here a halt was made and before work could be resumed the war came on and nothing further in the way of construction was possible.

The Houston men who had taken a leading part in the construction of this first railroad were W. M. Rice, W. A. Van Alstyne, James H. Stevens, B. A. Shepherd and W. J. Hutchins. These same men and others had organized a purely local company at Houston, one year before construction had begun on the Harrisburg road, and had obtained a charter under the name of the Brazos Plank Road. Their object was to grade a road from Houston to some point on the Brazos and then plank it over so as to enable the ox wagons, which were the only means of transportation in those days, to reach Houston easily at all seasons. That was in 1850, and the work of grading had extended the load twenty-three miles, though no planks had been laid, when some of the citizens of Chappell Hill, Washington County, issued a call for a great meeting to be held at Chappell Hill in the interest of building a railroad. Houston was invited to send delegates to that railroad convention, and a meeting was held in June, 1852, at the old Capitol Hotel for the purpose of discussing the question.

The meeting was largely attended and the stockholders in the Plank Road project were rather conspicuous among the other attendees. They had something of a double interest in the meeting for, while they knew the value of a railroad, they also knew that a railroad would completely destroy the value of their plank road. However, that fact seems not to have influenced their action, for they voted for sending a strong delegation to the Chappell Hill convention. This action was taken not without opposition, however, for while making no direct attack on the proposed railroad, Dr. Francis Moore, the editor of the *Telegraph*, made a vigorous fight for the plank road, which he argued was a present necessity and one which could be supplied at once, while it would take years to secure a charter for a railroad and again years to build the road after the charter was secured.

A fact worthy of special mention is that at that meeting Mr. Paul Bremond took a most prominent part in advocating the building of the railroad. This was his first appearance as a railroad advocate, and it deserves notice for it was he who was destined to become the real pioneer in railroad building in Texas. He had been one of the incorporators of the railroad chartered in 1848 under the name of the Galveston & Red River Railroad, which road, after many changes and amendments of its charter, finally became the Houston & Texas Central.

Mr. Bremond opposed adhering to the plank road if it was going to delay the building of the railroad and advocated speedy action on the latter proposition. The whole situation was gone over at that meeting with evident good results, for while neither the plank road nor the Washington County railroad was ever built, there was started a movement towards railroad building that resulted in work actually beginning on the Houston & Texas Central railroad on January 1, 1853. Mr. Paul Bremond had the honor of throwing the first shovel of dirt.

It may seem strange that anyone should have raised the least objection to railroad building at a time when the urgent need of a railroad was so obvious. That, however, may be explained by the fact that the Houston merchants had become used to the means of transit then in vogue, namely the ox-wagon, and had seen such good results following it that they were beginning to feel that they could do very well without other means of transportation. It must be borne in mind that the wagon service was not desultory nor intermittent. It was slow but it was certain and regular. For fourteen years it had been in force and was thoroughly organized. Its very magnitude and the numbers engaged in the business rendered the service almost continuous, and while individual teams might be subject to unreasonable detention and delay, there were so many others to take their place that such gaps were not noticeable.

As remarked, at the date of that Capitol Hotel meeting in 1852, the wagon service had been in force for fourteen years; had answered very well and met all conditions except that of speed. It is no wonder that the ox-team should have had its advocates at the meeting among those whose fortunes it had contributed so largely to build.

The service was indeed of great magnitude for it extended as far west as the Colorado River and up to Austin; as far as Waco to the northwest and to all points in East and Southern Central Texas. There were three or four thousand wagons engaged in the traffic and as each wagon required from sixteen to twenty-four oxen. When these numbers are considered, an idea of the amount of money involved may be formed. In those days every bale of cotton, every bushel of corn, every hide and everything else raised in Texas for the market came to Houston while all merchandise and groceries used in the interior, were hauled away from Houston by ox wagons. The business was a gigantic one.

But the success of starting the Buffalo Bayou & Colorado Railroad and of actually constructing 82 miles of it in 1852, was too great a demonstration of what could be done and it spurred the Houston people on, so that, as already remarked, Mr. Bremond actually threw the first shovel full of dirt for what was destined to become one of the greatest roads in the country, on January 1, 1853.

The story of Mr. Bremond's trials and tribulations has been told so often that it is needless to repeat it here. He accomplished something that was never accomplished before and has never been attempted since. He built fifty miles of good railroad on very little cash and a great deal of faith. He had absolute confidence in himself and in his own honesty and, somehow, he managed to inspire others with his own faith and confidence. He was the first railroad builder to water the stock of his road, but his method was different from that of his successors for he used faith, faith and then more faith, and that was all.

Mr. Bremond had hundreds of Irishmen working for him as section hands, and it is no exaggeration to say that before the expiration of the first six months he knew every one of them by sight, if not by name. This was not because of any great democracy on his part nor was it because of the prominence of good social qualities in him. It was based on something more reasonable and useful, for it was a measure of self-protection on his part. He used his knowledge of his men to enable him to keep from coming in contact with them. They were so unreasonable as to want pay for their work, and tiring of promises, they began to take matters in their own hands, with most unpleasant effects for Mr. Bremond.

No one ever knew how he accomplished it, but he actually built the road as far as Hempstead, fifty miles from Houston, with scarcely enough money to build ten miles, but with promises enough to have built the road to the North Pole. When the road reached Hempstead it struck a rich territory and began doing a large and lucrative business. Mr. Bremond's first care was to fulfill the promises he had made to his men, and their claims were the first that were settled. No man who ever trusted Paul Bremond, whether willingly or unwillingly, as those Irishmen did, ever lost a cent by doing so.

Twenty-three years later, in 1876, Mr. Bremond undertook the construction of another great road. He tried to get sufficient outside backing to enable him to build it without any of the friction and worry he had encountered with the Houston & Texas Central. His success in getting the financial aid he sought was only partial, but he had made up his mind to build the road and he did. Again he threw the first spadeful of dirt, and before he got through with his work, he had added the Houston East & West Texas Railroad to the iron ways centering at Houston.

When the war began Houston had made considerable progress in railroad building. The Texas & New Orleans had been constructed for about 111 miles, the Buffalo Bayou & Colorado had been extended to Alleyton, about 80 miles, and had been connected with Houston by the Columbia Tap road which extended from Houston to Columbia on the Brazos, 50 miles. The Houston & Texas Central had been extended to Millican, 81 miles from Houston, while the Galveston, Houston & Henderson road connected Houston and Galveston. The latter road was of the greatest military importance and was therefore kept up, in some way, during the four years of the war, but it was the only one. The other roads were, necessarily, allowed to go to ruin and when the war ended it was flattery to speak of them as "streaks of rust." The roadbed and right-of-way were about all that was left of them. The owners of the roads were in about as bad shape financially as were the roads physically, the result being that through reorganization and other methods, by 1870 virtually every railroad in Texas had changed hands.

With the completion of the Houston & Texas Central to Denison and its connection there with the Missouri, Kansas & Texas, thus forming a through line to St. Louis, the completion of the Texas & New Orleans line to New Orleans, and the extension of the Galveston, Houston and San Antonio to San Antonio, Houston became a railroad center at once. Then the International & Great Northern was built and, since the late seventies ,nearly each year has seen additions to Houston's railroads until now there are seventeen roads centering here and Houston is now one of the greatest railroad centers in the country.

It is interesting to note the difference in the railroad situation in Texas, and in Harris County, in particular, since the close of the war. As noted in the foregoing there were, at the close of the war, less than 370 miles of railroads in the whole State. Today Harris County alone has 450 miles within its limits, valued at $20,000,000, and, of this there is invested in terminal facilities at Houston about $12,000,000.

According to the most recent census report, there are 2,843 trainmen and clerks and 3,000 shopmen, or a total of 5,843 employees of the railroads paid off here. The total amount of their salaries and wages foot up $7,000,000 in round numbers. Really Mr. Bremond should be allowed to come back to life just to see what has grown from that first shovel of dirt he threw on that January morning in 1853.

The real importance and magnitude of the railroad situation is shown much better by the terminal facilities and trackage of the roads within the city limits. Placed end to end these sidetracks and switches would make a line of railroad 275 miles long, or just about the total length of the Houston & Texas Central Railroad.

The Houston yards of the Southern Pacific are the largest in the Southwest, with a trackage of 131 miles and a capacity of 10,000 cars. The Harriman tracks in Houston accommodate 123 different industrial plants, handle over 50,000 cars monthly and employ in that work 547 men. The roundhouses contain 72 stalls and 1,600 men are employed in the roundhouse and shops of this company. Twenty-two switch engines are kept constantly in use in these yards, taking cars to and from the industrial plants and in making up trains.

The Southern Pacific has 738 switches in the yards here. Among the other properties of the Southern Pacific are water tanks for the locomotives with a capacity of 100,000 gallons, and fuel oil tanks with a capacity of 225,000 barrels. The payroll of the Harriman interests in Houston is $4,000,000 annually.

The Houston Belt & Terminal Company's terminals aggregate trackage of about fifty-five miles. Among other properties of this company, in addition to the handsome passenger terminal and the convenient freight depots, are a roundhouse and machine shops, oil tanks and water tanks. Over 200 men are employed in these yards and shops. The company uses five switch engines, all of which burn oil. Practically every industrial plant in the city is reached by these tracks. The Houston Belt & Terminal company facilities are used by a number of the roads entering Houston. The Missouri, Kansas & Texas, the Santa Fe, the Trinity & Brazos Valley, the Frisco lines east and the Brownsville line all use the passenger station. The same lines, with the exception of the Katy, use the freight facilities.

The International & Great Northern has fifty-six miles of track in its local terminals. Its yards are mostly located on this side of the ship channel, though several miles are in the north side, where they touch a number of Houston industries. The principal shops of the company are located in Palestine, but fifty-seven men are employed in the repair shops here. About 120 other men are employed in the yards. The tracks of this company touch eighty-three different industrial plants. There are twelve switch engines operating in these yards, which accommodate 2,500 cars. The oil tanks of this company in Houston have a capacity of 190 barrels and the water tanks 75,000 gallons. There are six stalls in the roundhouse and 194 switches in the yards.

The Missouri, Kansas & Texas has about fifteen miles of track in its yards here. These yards have a capacity of 1,500 cars. Forty-three men are employed in the car department of the shops here and nine men are employed in the roundhouse, which has six stalls. In the yards there are forty-five men employed. Five switch engines are used in the yards constantly. The water tanks of this company here have a capacity of 100,000 gallons and the coal chutes forty tons.

The San Antonio & Aransas Pass has a yard track mileage of thirteen miles. Over 1,100 cars can be accommodated in them and three switch engines are necessary to handle the business. Nineteen men are employed in the yards. This company maintains a freight depot here, but its passenger trains enter the Southern Pacific depot. This company is also closely allied to the Southern Pacific and can touch most of the local industrial plants on the Harriman tracks.

All the other lines entering this city operate very little yard trackage, but have agreements with some one of these roads. The Galveston, Houston & Henderson and the Santa Fe both have small stretches of track here, but the mileage is small.

It must not be supposed that land transportation occupied the attention of the early Houstonians to the exclusion of everything else. Water transportation was given a great deal of attention, though in that direction not so much was required. There was plenty of water in the bayou to float the largest steamboats of that day, but there were one or two very troublesome features. There were obstacles to navigation near Morgan's Point, where there were two bars known as Red Fish and Clopper's bars. The water was shallow at these two points and whenever a severe norther blew the water out of Galveston Bay, these bars became impassable. At that time there was no remedy for the evil, so it was endured. At this end of the bayou there was a less formidable though serious obstacle. Between Houston and Harrisburg, for a distance by water of about sixteen miles, the bayou was very tortuous and overhung by large trees. The limbs of these trees played havoc with the woodwork of the steamboats and sometimes did serious damage to the boats themselves.

The work of improving navigation of the bayou was done exclusively by the people of Houston, without outside assistance. This is strange, for among the first measures passed by the Texas Congress was one setting aside $300,000 for the improvement of Texas rivers and harbors. For some unknown reason no request was ever made for this money and certainly not for the improvement of Buffalo Bayou. The work was rather crude and simple and consisted chiefly of cutting off overhanging limbs, removing sunken logs and cutting down trees that could be gotten rid of in no other way.

The importance of the bayou has always been recognized by Houstonians first, and then by the people of Texas and of the Southwest. In the early days it afforded the only safe communication between the people of Texas and the outside world, and in later days it has been made the basis for adjusting fair and equitable freight rates over the railroads. Aside from its importance as a freight carrier for Houston, it is important in regulating freights for the entire Southwest, and that fact creates interests in the bayou in territory remote from Houston. Buffalo Bayou should have pages devoted to it instead of this, necessarily, brief mention.

A year after Houston was laid out as a "city," the first steamboat, the *Laura*, came up here from Harrisburg, though she had a terrible time in accomplishing the passage from Harrisburg to Houston. The *Laura* seems to have cleared the bayou of so many obstructions that after that, several steamboats and sailing vessels came here and soon there was a regular service established between Houston and Galveston, which continued for some years after the war. The railroads finally destroyed the passenger business, and since then the immense traffic, amounting to millions each year, has been done by means of barges.

During the latter years there were some magnificent steamboats engaged in the Houston-Galveston trade, the two most magnificent ones being the *Diana* and *T. M. Bagby*, sister boats which compared favorably with any of the famous Mississippi river boats. They were each 170 feet long, 32 feet beam and five feet hold and were furnished in the most luxurious manner. Each was a veritable floating palace.

There are only stray pieces of records and statistics in existence relating to cotton shipments during early years. In 1839 only eight bales of cotton were shipped down the bayou. By 1844 those eight bales had grown to 7,000. The next year, 1845, a large cotton crop was made in Texas and the receipts and shipments here amounted to 12,000 bales. Nine years later they had grown to be 38,000 bales and the growth has been steady ever since. To-day Houston handles more actual spot cotton than any other market in America. The local sales of spot cotton in Houston average about 750,000 each season, while its receipts and shipments are between 2,500,000 and 3,000,000 bales yearly.

CHAPTER IV:
OF DOCTORS AND LAWYERS

Although there were such men as Ewing, Ashbel Smith, McAnally, and others of lesser prominence practicing medicine in the very early days of Houston there seems to have been no effort made by them to form a medical association. By the 1840s there were several additions to the profession. Among the newcomers were Dr. S. O. Young, Sr., Dr. William McCraven, Dr. W. D. Robinson, Dr. W H. Howard and Dr. L. A. Bryan.

Another decade passed before a successful attempt was made to form an association. In 1857 the first Houston medical association was organized. Dr. J. S. Duval was elected president; Dr. H. W. Waters, vice president and Dr. R. H. Boxley, secretary. The full membership consisted of J. S. Duval, W. H. Howard, Greenville Dowell, R. H. Boxley, and H. W. Waters. The objects of the organization were "to cultivate the science of medicine and all its collateral branches; to cherish and sustain medical character; to encourage medical etiquette and to promote mutual improvement, social intercourse and good feeling among members of the medical profession."

The first resolution adopted by the association was one aimed at the Homeopaths, and was as follows:

> Whereas, the scientific medical world has proven Homeopathy to be a species of empirism, too flagrant to merit the confidence of rational men, and too fabulous to deserve even the passing notice of an educated physician, and as we are convinced that it is a delusion, far surpassing any other ism known to the world, witchcraft not excepted, therefore we will not recognize, professionally or privately, any man who professes to cure diseases through the agency of Hahnemanic teachings.
>
> Be it Resolved, That as a diploma from a regularly organized medical school is the only evidence of qualification which our community can obtain in regard to the doctors in their midst, we respectfully recommend to the citizens of this flourishing city that they demand of every man who assumes the responsibility of a physician to their families, their diplomas as certificates of their worthiness of patronage, and that they see to it that they are not imposed on by a diploma from a medical society or a certificate of qualifications as a dresser in a hospital.

Two years later, in 1859, the Houston association issued a call addressed to the physicians of the State asking them to meet in Houston for the purpose of organizing a State Medical Association. There is reason to believe that such meeting was held but there is no record of it. The best evidence that there was such an association formed is the fact that Dr. W. H. Howard, who was a member of the City association in 1859, always spoke of the formation of the present State Medical Association as the re-organization of the old association.

The following named physicians met in the parlors of the Hutchins House on December 8, 1868, for the purpose of forming the Harris County Medical Association: L. A. Bryan, W. H. Howard, J. Larendon, D. F. Stuart, T. J. Poulson, R. W. Lunday, Alva Connell Sr., Alva Connell Jr., G. H. McDonnall, W. D. Robinson, T. J. Devereaux, J. M. Morris, W. P. Riddell.

After issuing a call to the physicians of Texas inviting them to meet in Houston on April 15, 1869 for the purpose of organizing, or rather re-organizing the State association, the Harris County association adjourned and never held another meeting until resurrected in 1904, since which date it has been one of the largest and most useful county associations in the State. The State Medical Association, however, was formed April 15, 1869 in the parlors of the Hutchins House.

If the early lawyers of Houston had any association they have left no record of the fact. There were great lawyers then and they set a standard of professional ethics and courtesy which, be it said to the credit of those who followed them, has never been lowered. From the earliest date the bar of Houston has always been great and influential. Among the big men when Houston was in its swaddling clothes were such men as Archibald Wynn, a criminal lawyer of marked ability; Peter W. Gray, W. P. Hamblen, E. A. Palmer, A. N. Jordan, J. W. Henderson, Benjamin F. Tankersley, Gus Tompkins, A. P. Thompson, A. S. Richardson and C. B. Sebin. The mere mention of these names is sufficient to show the high standing of the Houston bar at the very beginning.

During and after the close of the war there were many very brilliant and able lawyers who came to Houston. Among the most distinguished of these was Hon. Charles Stewart, D. U. Barziza, John H. Manley, Frank Spencer, George Goldthwaite, E. P. Hamblen, W. H. Crank, Judge Wilson, James Masterson, C. Anson Jones, son of the last President of the

Republic of Texas; W. A. Carrington, F. F. Chew, J. C. Hutchinson, Judge James Baker, W. B. Botts and others of equal prominence. As all know, these were men of the greatest probity and honor and would have reflected honor on any bar.

When the first amended constitution of Texas was adopted, it created a criminal district court for Harris and Galveston Counties. Judge Gustave Cook was appointed presiding judge and held the position for fourteen years. His successors on the bench have been C. L. Cleveland, E. D. Cavin, J. K. P. Gillaspie, E. R. Campbell and C. W. Robinson.

The following were the officers of the Eleventh District Court from its organization to the present day:

> 1837 to 1842—Benjamin C. Franklin, Judge; James S. Holman, Clerk; John W. Moore, Sheriff
>
> 1842 to 1849—Richard Morris, Judge; F. R. Lubbock, Clerk; M. T. Rogers, Sheriff
>
> 1849 to 1854—C. W. Buckley, Judge; F. R. Lubbock, Clerk; David Russell, Sheriff
>
> 1854 to 1862—Peter W. Gray, Judge
>
> 1862 to 1866—James A. Baker, Judge; W. B. Walker, Clerk; B. P. Lanham, Sheriff

From 1866 to 1869, during Reconstruction, there were no elections but the members of the bar selected George R. Scott, C. B. Sabin and P. W. Gray to act as judge of the court.

> 1869 to 1870—George R. Scott, Judge
>
> 1870 to 1892—James R. Masterson, Judge
>
> 1892 to 1896—S. H. Brashear, Judge
>
> 1896 to 1900—John G. Tod, Judge
>
> 1900 to date—Charles E. Ashe, Judge

The following is a complete list of the sheriffs of Harris County since the organization of the county to 1912:

> 1837-42—John W. Moore
>
> 1842-49—M. T. Rodgers

1849-54—David Russell

1854-58—Thomas Hogan

1858-62—M. M. Grimes

1862-66—B. P. Lanham

(Note: In 1866 John Proudfoot was elected sheriff but after holding office for a short time he disappeared. Mr. I. C. Lord, who was city marshal at the time, was appointed to act as sheriff until an election could be held. Another regular election was held and A. B. Hall was elected.)

1866-73—A. B. Hall

1873-76—S. S. Ashe

1876-82—Cornelius Noble

1882-86—John J. Fant

1886-94—George Ellis

1894-96—Fred Erichson

1896 to date—A. R. Anderson

The Fifty-first District Court was organized in 1897, and since then has had but three judges, the most recent of which are:

1902 to 1911—Judge Wm. P. Hamblen.

1911 to date—Judge William Masterson.

(Judge Hamblen died in office and Judge Masterson was appointed to succeed him.)

The Sixty-first District Court was organized in February of 1903, and has had but one presiding judge since its organization, Judge N. G. Kittrell.

The Harris County Court was created by the Legislature in 1867. John Brasher was elected county judge and served until 1869. His successor was Judge M. N. Brewster, who was put in office by the Republican reconstructionists. Judge Brewster was ousted by the Democrats in 1867 and Judge C. Anson Jones was elected. He served until his death in 1882. Judge E. P. Hamblen was elected in 1882 and served until 1884. Judge W. C. Andrews was elected in 1884 and served until 1892. Judge Andrews was a candidate for re-election in 1892, but died just before the election. On the death of Judge Andrews, Judge John G. Tod was placed on the ticket and was elected. In 1896, Judge W. N. Shaw was elected and remained in office for two years, being succeeded by Judge E. H. Vasmer in 1898. Judge Vasmer held office for four years and was followed by Judge Blake Dupree in 1902. Judge Dupree held office for two terms and was succeeded by Judge A. E. Amerman, the present incumbent.

The Corporation Court for Houston was created by act of the Legislature in 1899. Before the creation of this court, the city had a somewhat similar court. The presiding judge was sometimes the mayor, sometimes a recorder and at other times a justice of the peace. The method was so unsatisfactory that the present court was created to avoid all confusion. The first election to provide a judge for the new court was held soon after its creation. Judge A. R. Railey was elected and served until 1902, when he was defeated by Judge Marmion. When the form of the city government was changed, Judge Marmion was elected as one of the commissioners and Judge John H. Kirlicks was appointed to fill his unexpired term. He has held office ever since, much to the satisfaction of everybody except the evil-doers.

The Houston Bar Association was organized in 1870. Judge Peter W. Gray was its first president, Judge George Golthwaite its vice president and Col. Thomas J. Whitfield, recording secretary, N. P. Turner, correspond-ing secretary and W. C. Watson, treasurer. The Association was not nu-merically strong at the beginning, but it was strong in every other way, for among its members were some of the greatest lawyers in the country. Today the Association is strong in every way and compares favorably with similar associations anywhere. L. J. Bryan is president; Thomas H. Botts, secretary and Chester H. Bryan is treasurer. The Association has a membership of several hundred.

CHAPTER V:
THE PRINTED PAGE—EARLY HOUSTON NEWSPAPERS

Before the invasion of Texas by Santa Anna, there was a Mr. Gray who had a printing office consisting of a few fonts of type, a dilapidated press and a few other necessary things at Brazoria. From time to time he published a little news sheet, but made no effort to issue a regular newspaper. About the same time there was a little paper published at Nacogdoches, but it was spasmodic, irregular and not entitled to be considered a newspaper. With these two exceptions there was not a paper published in Texas prior to the Texas Revolution, nor while the Texans were striving to bring about concerted action against Mexico, except that established by the Borden Brothers, Gail and Thomas, at Columbia on October 10,1835. The Bordens had the greatest trouble getting not only material, but editors and printers, but finally they succeeded, and on the date named, issued the *Telegraph and Register*. Under the name of the *Telegraph* was destined to become and remain for years, the leading newspaper of Texas.

The *Telegraph and Register* was issued on the very day that the Texans, under Fannin, stormed and took Goliad, and as things began to happen with startling rapidity after that, there was no lack of sensational news for the paper. The paper was of the greatest assistance to the cause of the Texans, for it did much to concentrate public opinion and to keep the people informed about current events—information obtainable in no other way.

The paper was published regularly from October, 1835, until late in March, 1836, when the Bordens, learning that Houston had fallen back before Santa Anna and had crossed the Brazos at San Felipe, decided to fall back themselves and take their newspaper plant to a safer location. With great difficulty they managed to move everything to Harrisburg and had an issue of the *Telegraph* all ready for the press when Santa Anna's soldiers showed up, burned their building and threw their press into the bayou.

Instead of being discouraged, the Bordens ordered a new outfit from Cincinnati, and, sometime in August, 1836, resumed the publication of the *Telegraph* in Columbia, where the Texas Congress met two months later. Gail Borden had been appointed collector of customs at Galveston and it was necessary for him to make his home there. So he retired from the *Telegraph* and since his brother Tom wished to leave also, they sold the paper to Mr. Jacob Cruger and Dr. Francis Moore, who moved it to Houston and issued the first number here on May 2, 1837. Dr. Moore was chief editor of the *Telegraph* until 1853, when Harry H. Allen became editor and proprietor. In 1856, he sold the paper to Mr. E. H. Cushing, one of the most gifted writers and able newspapermen the state has ever had.

Ten years later, in 1866, Mr. Cushing sold the *Telegraph* to Col. C. C. Gillespie, who was a strong and forcible writer but rather a poor editor. Col. Gillespie employed Mr. J. E. Carnes as editorial writer and between the two, the *Telegraph* soon became the leading literary paper of the state. Too much attention was paid to fine writing and too little to news, so the paper lost ground and was about on its last legs when Col. Gillespie sold it to General Webb, who published it regularly until 1873, when the financial panic of that year killed it.

The next year Mr. A. C. Gray revived it and, under his able management, it soon became the leading paper of the state again. In its first issue under his management, April 16, 1874, Mr. Gray said:

> *The Houston Telegraph* is an old and familiar friend to very many in and out of Texas who will hail its reappearance as the return of an old, a much loved and greatly lamented companion. Founded in the days of the Republic, it was true to the government and to the people, and, by its efforts, accomplished perhaps as much as any other instrumentality in calling attention to and developing the resources of this great commonwealth. Under the control and guidance of such men as Gail Borden, Dr. Francis Moore, Henry Allen, E. H. Cushing and others, it has reared for itself an imperishable monument, by its fidelity to the law, good government and general progress.
>
> It is with no ordinary satisfaction, and we trust a pardonable pride, that the present managing editor and proprietor refers to his past connection with and present relation to the office of the *Telegraph*. Twenty-eight years ago, when a mere boy, he entered it as an apprentice. By patient toil and proper pride in his chosen profession he became its business manager during its most prosperous period. And when, under the financial panic of 1873, it was forced to suspend and ceased to make its daily appearance, he mourned it as if a friend had fallen. Since then it has been his ambition to call the slumbering Ajax to the field again and bid it battle with renewed energy for constitutional government, Democratic principles and the general weal.

Mr. Gray made a magnificent fight to reinstate the *Telegraph* in the front ranks of Texas journals. From a literary and politically influential point of view he was successful, but the financial strain became too great. In 1878 the *Telegraph* was forced to cease publication and its pages were closed forever.

In the early fifties a Mr. Cruger (not the Cruger who was associated with Dr. Moore on the *Telegraph* when it was established in Houston) began the publication of a tri-weekly paper called *The Morning Star*. This appears to have been quite an ambitious and prominent paper, judging by the incomplete files of it now in the Carnegie Library.

It seems that everybody wanted to start a newspaper in Houston after the war, for between 1865 and 1880 there were no less than twenty-one that had appeared, splashed about in the troubled waters of journalism and then sunk beneath the waves to rise no more. Some of them were worthy and deserving papers, but the majority of them were catch penny affairs that were started on a shoestring, merely to get hold of a little cash from a confiding public.

An exception was the *Houston Age*, owned later by Mr. Fourmy, the Directory man at present associated with Mr. Morrison. The *Age* became famous under the editorial management of Major Dan McGary, and also through the caustic articles contributed by Col. Dick Westcott during heated political campaigns, and all campaigns were heated during the existence of the *Age*.

In 1880, Mr. Gail Johnson, a grandson of Mr. Gail Borden, the founder of the old *Telegraph*, established the *Houston Post*. This paper had ample financial backing and an able, well-organized editorial and business force. It was a bright, newsy paper and soon secured a strong foothold in Houston and throughout the state as well. There is no question that it would have ultimately become one of the leading papers of the state but for a fatal error committed by Judge Johnson, the father of Mr. Gail Johnson. The Judge was an ardent Republican and conceived an idea that he could make the *Post* a power in politics by supporting a candidate against the regular nominee of the Democratic party.

The Judge lost sight of the fact that Texas had so recently emerged from the Reconstruction, scalawag rule that had cursed the state, and that the average citizen associated the name "Republican" with all that was despicable and contemptible. Judge John Ireland was the regular Democratic nominee and he was opposed by Col. Wash Jones, who ran as an independent candidate. The *Post* supported Jones, and did so in such a masterly manner as to attract attention and cause a demand for the paper. The circulation increased rapidly and continued to increase until the day of election. Then Ireland was triumphantly elected and the bubble burst. The circulation dropped off more rapidly than it had increased. The paper had lots of money behind it, however, and continued its career just as though nothing had occurred to mar the serenity of its course.

Mr. Gail Johnson had grown disgusted and had disposed of his interest to his father, who in 1883 sold the *Post* to a syndicate of Houston capitalists, who had conceived the idea of converting it into a great Democratic State paper. They secured the services of Mr. Hardenbrook, an experienced newspaperman, and placed him in full charge, supplying him with plenty of money and giving him a free hand to do as he chose. Hardenbrook brought Mr. Tobe Mitchell from St. Louis and placed him in charge of the editorial room. Hardenbrook and Mitchell spent money freely and soon made the *Post* one of the leading papers of the South. In eight or nine months they spent very nearly $300,000. Then the backers of the paper became alarmed and, one by one, withdrew. Then the crash came and the paper suspended publication suddenly.

The suspension of the *Post* left Houston without a morning paper and, to remedy the defect, Dr. S. O. Young (your humble author) organized a company composed of practical printers and newspapermen and began the publication of a morning paper which was called the *Houston Chronicle*. Mr. Baker, who now owned the *Post* plant, allowed the company to use it and also allowed them to use the large supply of paper the *Post* had on hand when it suspended, charging only for what was actually used at cost. The *Chronicle* was not a brilliant sheet, but it was an honest and fairly good paper. It was run strictly on the pay-as-you-go principle and at the end of its first year, it had an empty treasury but it did not owe a dollar to anyone.

After an existence of very nearly eighteen months Dr. Young, who had secured entire control of the *Chronicle*, merged it with the *Journal*, an afternoon paper owned by Professor Girardeau and Mr. J. L. Watson. The *Journal* ceased publication and the new morning paper was called the *Houston Daily Post*.

The first issue of the *Post* was on April 5, 1885. Effort was made to publish a more pretentious paper than the *Chronicle* had been, but that increased the expense so much so that serious complications arose. Professor Girardeau became disgusted and turned his back on journalism. Messrs. Young and Watson purchased his interest and continued the struggle. The loss to the paper of such a man as Professor Girardeau was a serious embarrassment. However, it was a blessing in disguise, for the gentlemen were enabled to secure Col. R. M. Johnston as editorial manager, and Colonel Johnston is one of the best and most practical newspapermen in the country.

In September of the same year, Dr. Young received a flattering offer from the *Galveston News* to become one of its editorial writers. He gave his interest in the *Post* to Messrs. Watson and Johnston and went to Galveston. This left Watson and Johnston sole proprietors of the *Post*. They managed to keep their heads above water for about a year and in 1886, they reorganized the *Post*, turning it into a stock company. Even after that the *Post* had uphill sailing for a year or two, but finally the magnificent ability of Colonel Johnston as an editorial manager, backed by the absolute genius of Watson in the business office, began to tell and the *Post* became what it is today, one of the great newspapers of the Southwest.

Mr. W. H. Bailey, a bright young newspaperman, began the publication of an afternoon paper called the *Herald*. This was a regular live wire and was fully charged all the time. Mr. Bailey believed in telling the truth all the time regardless of whom the truth might be about and he did so in every issue of the *Herald*. No one was too high and prominent to escape criticism and censure if he deserved them. Bailey played no favorites, but went after wrong-doers wherever discovered. The result was almost continual warfare for the first few months of the *Herald's* existence, and, what was more to the editor's satisfaction, an immense circulation for the paper. Subscriptions and advertisements poured in and the *Herald* became one of the leading papers in South Texas.

After a red-hot existence of eighteen years the *Herald* was finally sold to Mr. M. E. Foster, who had organized the *Houston Chronicle* and who bought the plant and good will of the *Herald*. The *Houston Chronicle* began publication on October 14, 1901, and it is no exaggeration to say that it was a success from its very first issue. Its editor and proprietor, Mr. M. E. Foster, was no novice, having been managing editor of the *Houston Post* and having had large experience and training. He has made the *Chronicle* one of the leading state papers and its influence is great both in Houston and throughout the state.

On May 18, 1880, a number of Texas editors assembled in the parlor of the Hutchins House and organized the Texas Press Association. For four years the Association met in Houston and then determined to meet each year in a different city. From a mere handful of members at the beginning, the Association has grown to be one of the largest and most important in the South and its annual meetings are looked forward to with pleasurable anticipation by the members for they are always most profitable and enjoyable.

CHAPTER VI:
ENGINES OF FINANCE

Mr. T. W. House, Sr., Mr. W. J. Hutchins, Mr. Cornelius Ennis and others of the early merchants carried on banking affairs of their own in connection with their cotton and mercantile businesses, extending credit to customers. In 1854, Mr. B. A. Shepherd opened an independent bank, engaging exclusively in the banking business. This was the first bank in Houston and Mr. Shepherd was the first genuine banker.

In 1873 Mr. Hutchins ceased banking activities and devoted himself solely to his wholesale business. Mr. House reversed Mr. Hutchins' process in part, for while he did not close out his cotton and wholesale business, he separated them from his banking activities and gave the latter more of his attention. When Mr. House died in 1881, his oldest son, T. W. House, Jr., bought the interests of his brothers in the bank and devoted his whole time to its affairs. House's bank soon became one of the greatest financial institutions in the state. During the great panic of 1907, due to many complications and circumstances, it was forced to close its doors.

The City Bank of Houston began business November 1, 1870, with a capital stock of $250,000. It did business for fifteen years, but in 1885 was forced to suspend payment and went into the hands of a receiver. The Houston Savings Bank, organized in 1874, suspended payment and closed its doors in 1886. The public lost very little money by the failure of this bank or by that of the City Bank, which had occurred the year before.

The First National Bank was organized in 1866 by Mr. B. A. Shepherd and Mr. T. M. Bagby, the latter being its first president. On the death of Mr. Bagby, Mr. Shepherd became president and when he died his son-in-law, Mr. A. S. Root, succeeded him. A few years ago Mr. Root died and Mr. O. L. Cochran, another son-in-law of Mr. Shepherd, became and is still president.

This bank is one of the strongest institutions in the country. Its original capital was $100,000. In 1906 this was increased to $500,000. In 1909 the stock was again doubled and in 1912 it was increased to $2,000,000. Its business has also shown a phenomenal growth, having about doubled in three years. September 1, 1909, its deposits were $4,764,967. September 1, 1910, the deposits had grown to $6,421,938. Four months later, January 7, 1911, they were $7,953,096. Just two months later, March 7, 1911, they were $8,432,907. On April 18, 1912, deposits were slightly under $9,000,000, or to be exact, $8,973,999.80.

The home of this bank is one of the handsomest buildings in the city. It is only eight stories high, but it has an immense floor space, larger than any bank in the South. It has a fine frontage on Main Street and runs back for more than half a block on Franklin Avenue. In addition to this, it has an ell that extends from the Franklin side far back towards the middle of the block. The entire first, or ground floor is used by the bank while the other seven stories are used as offices. The building is of reinforced concrete, steel structure and is fireproof in every way. It has its own water supply, derived from a large artesian well. It also has its own heating and electric light plant. There are three large and rapid elevators, and the building is equipped from top to bottom with every device that contributes to the comfort and convenience of its tenants.

It was exactly twenty years after the organization of the First National Bank before another was organized. This was the Commercial National Bank, organized in 1886, with a capital stock of $500,000. This bank did an immense business and had large deposits. It was recently merged with the South Texas National Bank.

The Houston National was the third national bank organized in Houston. It was chartered in 1889, but in 1909 obtained a new charter under the name of the Houston National Exchange Bank. This bank has a most extraordinary record. Its capital stock is only $200,000, while its surplus and undivided profits amount to three-fourths of its capital stock. It has deposits of very nearly four million dollars. The officers of the Houston National Exchange Bank are Joseph F. Meyer, president; M. M. Graves, vice president; Henry S. Fox, Jr., active vice president; Joseph W. Hertford, cashier; F. F. Dearing and W. B. Hilliard, assistant cashiers.

The South Texas National Bank was the fourth national bank organized in Houston. It obtained its charter in 1890. On March 2, 1912, the South Texas National Bank absorbed the Texas Commercial National Bank. The new bank thus formed became the South Texas Commercial National Bank, with a capital of $1,000,000. Nineteen days after the consolidation the deposits of the new bank were $11,000,000, while the capital and surplus amounted to nearly $2,000,000.

The home of this bank is one of the finest and, architecturally, most beautiful buildings in the South. The front of the building is perfectly plain, but is of the purest marble. There are four columns supporting the main pediment, each turned from a solid slab of marble, the shafts of each being twenty-two feet long. The interior of the building is more beautiful than its exterior. Only the finest marble and ornamental bronze were used in the interior finish and the result is most pleasing. The high arched ceiling is an attractive feature. Only the very best artists and superior workers were employed in finishing this building and the results obtained by them speak volumes for their taste and skill.

The following are the officers of the South Texas Commercial National Bank: Chairman of the board, Charles Dillingham; president, W. B. Chew; active vice president and cashier, B. D. Harris; vice presidents, James A. Baker, John M. Dorrance, J. E. McAshan, Thornwell Fay and Judge T. J. Freeman. Assistant cashiers, August De Zavalla, P. J. Evershade, Paul G. Taylor.

There are twenty-five directors, being the directors of the two consolidated banks. They are James A. Baker, F. A. Heitmann, Conrad Bering, O. T. Holt, R. Lee Blaffer, R. S. Lovett, Horace Booth, H. F. McGregor, Chester H. Bryan, J. E. McAshan, W. B. Chew, C. H. Markham, James D. Dawson, J. V. Neuhaus, Charles Dillingham, Edwin B. Parker, John M. Dorrance, S. C. Red, Thornwell Fay, Daniel Ripley, Thomas J. Freeman, Cleveland Sewall, B. D. Harris, J. J. Settegast, Jr .

Houston's fifth national bank was the Union National Bank, organized in 1905. This bank represents three original banks. The Union Bank and Trust Company was chartered in 1905. In 1908, it absorbed the Merchants National Bank. When this was done the bank took its present name and was chartered as the Union National Bank with a capital of $1,000,000. This bank is one of the strongest banks in the South and does an immense business. The twelve-story steel, reinforced concrete, granite and brick building of this bank is one of the finest and most attractive buildings in the city. There are twelve stories above ground and an immense basement. The basement and ground floor are used exclusively by the bank, while the other stories are devoted to modern offices. The basement is fitted up as elegantly as other parts of the building and, besides the huge vaults, contains private rooms for the patrons of the bank. There are safety vaults and store rooms for the safe keeping of bulky valuables.

The building is entirely independent of all outside utilities, having its own artesian water supply, its own heating and electric light plant and its

own chilled air system for use in the summer. There are several large elevators in the building, making access to every floor an easy thing. Including
the ground the building cost almost exactly $1,000,000. The officers of the
Union National Bank are: J. S. Rice, president; T. C. Dunn, George Ham-
men, W. T. Carter, Abe Levy, J. M. Rockwell, Jesse H. Jones and C. G.
Pillot, vice presidents; DeWitt C. Dunn, cashier; D. W. Cooley and H. B.
Finch, assistant cashiers.

Houston's youngest national bank, the Lumbermans National, seems to
have been something of an absorber and consolidator itself. It was organized
and chartered in 1907 with a capital of $400,000. In 1909, it absorbed the
National City Bank, and the next year the American National Bank and
Trust Company liquidated and turned over its business to the Lumbermans
Bank. This bank is one of the strong financial institutions of Houston and
of South Texas, and does an immense business. The officers of the Lumbermans National Bank are S. F. Carter, president; Guy M. Bryan, active vice
president; H. M. Garwood and W. D. Cleveland, vice presidents; Lynn P.
Talley, cashier; M. S. Murray and H. M. Wilkens, assistant cashiers.

The fact that Houston is the real financial center of the State is shown by
the report of the Treasury Department in Washington issued February 20,
1912. In the report the standing of six leading cities is given and Houston
occupies first place with a wide margin over her nearest competitor, Dallas.

	Loans & Discounts	Lawful Reserves	Individual Deposits
Houston	$22,628,110	$3,728,112	$22,425,250
Dallas	$17,221,605	$2,021,996	$17,556,376
Fort Worth	$12,277,281	$1,277,660	$10,237,269
San Antonio	$9,073,658	$1,716,011	$9,105,007
Waco	$5,832,276	$711,567	$5,113,521
Galveston	$3,901,517	$764,253	$3,609,664

The foregoing pages tell of Houston's financial strength, but they tell only
one-half of the story. Banks represent the commercial and business life of
a community, their condition giving in concise form the extent and volume
of trade in a way that can be understood by all. In the very nature of things,
banks, no matter how great and strong, cannot add to the physical and ma-

terial growth of a community except indirectly. Banks prosper by lending money for short periods on commercial paper and similar securities. Their collateral must be such as can be easily turned into cash on short notice. Lands, mortgages, vendors lien notes and such things, considered gilt edge securities the world over, are not so considered by banks. The law even goes so far as to prohibit national banks taking land as security for loans.

It is for the purpose of handling just such business as the banks cannot or will not handle, that trust companies are formed. There is an indirect community of interest between the banks and trust companies, but there are no conflicting interests. One represents the financial and trade conditions of the community while the other represents the material growth, expansion and development of the community. No bank is willing to undertake to do the many things that modern business methods demand shall be done. Such things are entirely without the province of banks. It is for the purpose of doing these things that trust companies have been formed. The trust companies perform a dual duty. They care for and conserve estates placed in their charge, and they also afford a source from which may be obtained long-term loans. Usually these loans are made for the purpose of improving and developing intrinsically valuable property with the property itself taken as security for payment of the debt. The length of the loan, the rate of interest paid by the borrower and the absolute security afforded by the property held as collateral make such a transaction a safe and sure investment for the trust company. The reasonable interest paid by the borrower and the long time given him in which to pay back the loan make the transaction a very advantageous one for the borrower.

The wonderful growth of Houston during the last seven or eight years has led to the formation of trust companies here and Houston now has several of the strongest in the South. The oldest trust company in Texas was organized in Houston thirty-seven years ago, in 1875. The history of those dark and stormy days would lead one to think that large financial schemes would have no place in them, and yet the Houston Land and Trust Company was chartered during the darkest days of the city. It was originally chartered as a land and trust company and did only a small and unimportant business for years. In 1889 it was reorganized and took out a new charter which enabled it to do a regular trust and mortgage business. It is now one of the most important institutions of its kind in the country and does an immense and highly profitable business. Its business is strictly that of a trust company and in no way does it encroach on the business done by banks. The following was the condition of this company at the close of business, March 31, 1912:

Capital stock	$250,000.00
Surplus	$340,000.00
Undivided profits	$2,980.00
Time certificates of deposit	$1,313,364.44
Accrued interest payable	$13,063.66
Estate and trust account	$104,827.27
Dividend #36, payable 5/1/1912	$7,500.00
	$2,031,735.37

The officers of Houston Land and Trust are O. L. Cochran, president; R. E. Paine, vice president; P. B. Timpson, vice president; W. S. Patton, secretary and treasurer; O. R. Weyrich, assistant secretary.

The Southern Trust Company was organized in 1909 and began business in January, 1910. Its capital stock was $500,000 but this was almost immediately increased to $800,000. The success of this company has been phenomenal. It is only a little over two years old and yet it has earned over half a million dollars and has paid large dividends since its organization. Following is the statement of this company at the close of business April 18, 1912:

Capital stock	$800,000.00
Surplus	$400,000.00
Undivided profits	$168,278.21
Trust funds	$6,466.10
Reserved for taxes, 1912	$4,500.00
Bills payable and rediscounts	$140,000.00
Certificates of deposit	$177,300.00
Accounts payable	$2,438.28
	$1,698,982.59

The officers of the Southern Trust Company are James L. Autry, president; Travis Holland, vice president; J. W. Powers, Jr., secretary; Beverly W. Ward, assistant secretary; Ernest Carroll, treasurer.

The Texas Trust Company was organized in 1909 with a capital stock of $500,000. It at once established for itself a reputation for soundness and conservatism, which made at once towards its success. The company was in active operation for slightly over two years and during that time paid dividends of 10 per cent and accumulated a surplus of very nearly a quarter of a million dollars. On September 1, 1911, the Texas Trust Company consolidated with the Bankers' Trust Company, thus making the latter one of the greatest trust companies in the South.

The Bankers' Trust Company was chartered in 1909 with a capital stock of $500,000, and a paid in surplus of $25,000. The capital stock was soon increased to $1,000,000. The volume of business done by this company was very great and its success was phenomenal. September 1, 1911, the Bankers' Trust Company absorbed the Texas Trust Company, at the same time increasing its capital stock to $2,000,000. This company transacts a general trust business and is fully equipped in all its departments to meet the financial requirements of its patrons. It takes charge of real and personal estates, and acts as executor, administrator, receiver and trustee. Following is the statement of this company, issued at the close of business April 18, 1912:

Capital stock	$2,000,000.00
Surplus and profits	$881,638.23
Reserved for taxes	$12,000.00
Demand deposits	$44,102.35
Certificates of deposit	$723,496.21
Cashier's checks	$4,302.00
Trust funds	$900,992.46
Rediscounts	$12,973.35
	$4,579,504.35

The officers of the Bankers' Trust Company are Jesse H. Jones, chairman of the board; J. S. Rice, president; Tom M. Taylor, N. E. Meador, J. M. Rockwell, James A. Baker, A. M. Levy, W. T. Carter, C. G. Pillot and J. W. Link, vice presidents; C. M. Malone, secretary; F. J. Heyne, treasurer and cashier; Burke Baker, bond officer; William Malone, real estate officer; Andrews, Ball & Streetman, counsel.

The American Trust Company is a young affair, being only about a year old. It was organized in 1911 with a capital stock of $500,000. This company has banking privileges and intends on taking full advantage of them. Its business at present is both bank and trust business and it bids fair to be one of the strong financial institutions of Houston, both as a bank and as a trust company. Its officers are J. D. Hefley, president; J. E. Duff, vice president; N. B. Sligh, treasurer.

The Commonwealth Trust Company is Houston's latest trust company. It has just been organized and has not yet opened its doors for business. Its capital stock of $500,000 has been over-subscribed. Its charter is one of wide scope and gives it large privileges and an ample field of operation. The charter is that of the First State Bank of Hillsboro, Texas. Mr. W. E. Richards, the president of the present trust company, purchased the Hillsboro charter and at once organized The Commonwealth Trust Company. The officers of the company are W. E. Richards, president; Exile Burkitt, active vice president; Horace Booth, Geo. W. Riddle, W. R. Allison, Monta J. Moore, W. H. Gill, H. H. Simmons, John H. Foster, John S. Callaway and R. E. Burt, directors.

The Continental Trust Company is now in process of organization here in Houston. This is to be one of the greatest and most powerful trust companies in the country. The capital stock of the company will be $1,000,000, while there will also be a paid-in surplus of $1,000,000. The prospectus of this company gives so clear an idea of the functions of a trust company, and particularly of the objects of the present company, that the following liberal extract is taken from it:

> The Continental Trust Company (without banking privileges) of Houston, Texas, has been organized to assist in supplying the urgent demand for a place of sufficient magnitude and strength to which application may be made for absolutely good first mortgage or vendor's lien loans; where persons seeking investments may expect to find good securities in amounts commensurate with their respective means available for employment; being a medium where the borrower and investor come together; also where reliable information concerning relative values of property may be obtained with a view of creating closer relations with Eastern and foreign connections to the end of filling a distinct need incident to the upbuilding of a country already demonstrated to be resourceful and rapidly increasing in wealth.

Practically every city in Texas is experiencing a large demand for gilt-edge first mortgage and vendor's lien loans, and trust companies in Texas, which are only a few in number, are unable to supply but a small percentage of such demand...The powers which the company will exercise are those of the soundest institutions of this character, omitting banking functions, and especially the receipt of deposits subject to check. It will act chiefly as intermediary between the investor and the borrower, between capital and those who need capital to develop the resources of Texas. Its profits will be derived from expert service which it will offer the investor, together with the assurance of its large financial responsibility in placing and safeguarding funds; and to those needing capital, by furnishing a market for securities and rendering assistance necessary to place them in such form as will make them marketable.

Mr. S. F. Carter, president of the Lumbermans National Bank; Hon. Jonathan Lane, Mr. John H. Thompson, vice president and general manager of the Guarantee Life Insurance Company of Houston; Mr. James F. Sadler, Jr., and other business associates of these gentlemen are prominent in organizing this company, so it is quite evident that its success is assured.

CHAPTER VII:
GOD'S HOUSE ON THE BAYOU

When the Allens laid out Houston they set aside the quarter of a block on the northwest corner of Capitol and Main "for church purposes." The gift was to no denomination or sect, but was to all. A year or two later there was a small building erected on one of the lots and all denominations had the use of it. After the State House was built, religious services were held in one of its halls.

Legend says that the first religious service ever held in Houston was under the spreading branches of a tree that grew on Market Square, in 1837, but the fact remains that the first authentic evangelical service was that which occurred in 1836. The fact is a matter of record that Rev. Mr. Morrell, an itinerant Baptist preacher who came to Texas before San Jacinto, preached in Houston in 1836.

It is rather singular that with all the "hard cases" that were in Houston in the early days, and the consequent necessity for taking precautions for controlling them, the first vigilance committee formed in Houston should have been composed entirely of preachers and that the object of the committee should have been to guard the public against being imposed on by fraudulent preachers. Such was the case and the Preachers' Vigilance Committee was formed in May of 1837. There is no record of their stomping out any frauds, or of anything else they did. No doubt their very existence warned away frauds and thus accomplished what they desired without further exertion on their part.

The first church to secure a permanent foothold in Houston was the Methodist, which perfected an organization in 1837. That year the Allens donated to the Methodist brethren the half block on the north side of Texas Avenue between Travis and Milam Streets.

The establishment of Methodism here was almost entirely the work of one individual, the late honored and revered Charles Shearn. Mr. Shearn was a most earnest and devout Christian who devoted his life to the advancement of his church. He brought from New Orleans, at his personal expense, a minister of the gospel, gave him a home in his own house, and was mainly responsible for the establishment, growth and influence of the Methodist church here. In later years he gave largely, both in time and money, to the church cause and after the war he built, almost entirely with his own money, the church on Texas Avenue, afterwards torn down when the site was sold.

The valuable property on Texas Avenue was disposed of, and the congregation, now flush with money, was determined to build an imposing edifice. They put up a magnificent building on Main Street and so far forgot their old benefactor, in the days of their prosperity, that his name was dropped entirely. Shearn Church thus became the First Methodist Church. The writer is not a member of the Methodist church, and probably it is a bit of impertinence for him to express an opinion on the subject, but the temptation is simply too strong to resist. The dropping of the name of the good old saint who did so much for the church and who, unaided and almost alone, placed it on its feet and guided it on the way to prosperity, was an act by the side of which the proverbial ingratitude of republics sinks into insignificance.

The First Presbyterian Church was organized in the Senate chamber of the Capitol building in 1838. Though a church organization was perfected in 1838, no effort was made to erect a church building until 1843. One reason for the delay was, no doubt, the fact that the Allens had stipulated that all churches should have free use of the site on Capitol and Main until they secured building sites of their own, when the property should revert to the Presbyterians for their sole use. Although, by 1843, all the various churches did not have permanent homes of their own, most of them were making active efforts to secure them, so the Presbyterians determined to build. Early in the year a canvass was made, funds secured, and by the end of the year the First Presbyterian church was erected on Main Street near the corner of Capitol. It was a large frame building, facing Main Street, and was used by the congregation for many years until it was destroyed by fire in 1859.

When the congregation erected a new building they used brick and faced the church on Capitol Street. Services were held there until, in 1879, the building cracked badly and was declared to be unsafe. The building was torn down and restored, thus making it safe. The congregation moved into their restored building early in 1880. The first sermon was preached by their new pastor, Rev. E. D. Junkin, who in addition to being a most eloquent and Christian gentleman, had the distinction of being the brother-in-law of the famous Confederate General Stonewall Jackson. Dr. Junkin's successor was Rev. Dr. Wm. Hayne Leavell. Dr. Leavell resigned in 1906 and was succeeded by the Rev. Dr. Wm. States Jacobs, the present pastor.

The Presbyterians have had fewer pastors than any of the other churches, yet few as they have had, they have lost two by sea tragedies. In 1858 Rev. Mr. Ruthvan was lost at sea. He was going from Galveston to New Orleans on the ill-fated *Nautilus*, which was lost in a great storm that swept the gulf. All the passengers and crew were lost with the exception of a negro deck hand, who clung to a bale of cotton and was picked up by a passing vessel a day or two later. In 1866, Rev. Dr. Castleton and his wife took passage out of Galveston in a sailing vessel. From that day to this not a word has been heard from them, nor has a trace of the vessel ever been found.

The Episcopal church was organized in 1839, and had a fairly good congregation at the very start, since there were thirty-nine adherents of that denomination present at the initial meeting. The early services were conducted by laymen and an occasional itinerant minister, until 1845, when the members adopted a constitution, took the name of Christ Church and determined to erect a house of worship. The cornerstone for the new building was laid in 1846 and the building was consecrated by Bishop Freeman, Bishop of Louisiana, May 9, 1847. There was no regular pastor of Christ Church for several years, but services were held regularly, lay members and an occasional minister officiating.

The old church was torn down and another erected on its site in 1859. In 1876 that building was torn down to make place for a third church, which in turn was demolished in 1893, when the cornerstone of the present beautiful building was laid. Christ Church runs the Methodist a close race in the rapid change of pastors, for up to 1892 there had been no less than fifteen regular pastors. That year, however, something like permanency was established and Rev. Dr. Henry D. Aves took charge of the affairs of the church, both spiritual and temporal. Its great prosperity dates from his installation in office and during the years of his incumbency the most marvelous growth and expansion were shown. Dr. Aves became Bishop of Mexico and was succeeded by Rev. Dr. Peter Gray Sears, who has shown himself to be a worthy successor.

The First Baptist Church of Houston was organized April 10, 1841. The history of this church is interesting, for unlike that of the others, its inception was the result of the untiring efforts of two Christian women, Mrs. C. M. Fuller and Mrs. Piety L. Hadley. Soon after the organization of the church, these ladies undertook to buy ground and erect a church building. They had no money and met with small encouragement even from their fellow church members and members of their own families. Someone, as a joke, gave them a rawboned mule. This they fattened and sold, thus securing a nucleus for a building fund. They then gave a fair where homemade useful articles were sold. The fair and the mule brought them in $450. Then they gave another fair, larger than the other, and secured an additional $900.

With this money they purchased the lots on the corner of Texas Avenue and Travis Street, where the Milby Hotel now stands. During all their labors these ladies had the untiring assistance of good old Brother Pilgrim, a pious and devout Christian gentleman. After purchasing the lots, the ladies wrote to Rev. William Tryan and asked him to come and take charge of the church, which numbered seventeen members. Dr. Tryan accepted the call, came to Houston, and it was through his effort that sufficient money was obtained to build the first Baptist church, which stood for many years on the southeast corner of Texas Avenue and Travis Street. In 1883 the property was sold and a new church was erected in 1883-84. This church was destroyed by the great storm in 1900 and another was erected on the corner of Fannin and Walker in 1903. Rev. Dr. J. L. Gross is the present pastor of this church.

There were Catholic missionaries here in the very early days of Houston's existence, but no effort was made to establish a regularly organized church and to erect a building until 1841, when a French priest, Rev. Father Querat, purchased the quarter block on the south side of Franklin Avenue and Caroline Street. Through his efforts sufficient money was obtained to put up a small wooden building and to build another for a schoolhouse and home for the priest. For many years this little church was used and not until 1869 was an effort made to secure larger quarters. In 1869 the old church property was sold and a block of ground on Texas Avenue and Crawford Street was purchased. In 1871 the new church was completed and has been occupied ever since. The handsome brick building known as the Church of the Annunciation, and is one of the most beautiful churches in the city. Father Hennessy was pastor at the time and has been such all these years, honored and respected by both Catholics and Protestants. The whole block is used by the church, the church edifice occupying the northwest side, while the remainder is given over to elegant school and priest houses.

The first German Lutheran church was organized in Houston either in 1851 or 1852. This tardy organization is somewhat difficult to understand, since there were so many Germans among the early citizens of Houston. In 1853 the church purchased the northwest corner of the block on Texas Avenue and Milam Street and erected a very large and imposing frame building on the corner lot. Rev. Mr. Braun was the pastor, and he also conducted a fine German and English school, using the church building for that purpose. Among the members of this church were some of the most prominent and useful German citizens of Houston. About 1875 a second Lutheran church was built on Louisiana between Prairie and Preston. Some years later both the first and second sites were sold and new churches erected elsewhere, one on Texas Avenue and Caroline Street and the other on Washington and Young Avenue.

From the earliest days of Houston's existence until in the early sixties, the Hebrew congregation in this city was kept intact through the personal exertions of Father Levy, as the venerable rabbi was called. He was a man of great force of character and was honored and respected by everybody irrespective of creed or belief. After his death the office was filled by a most worthy successor, Rabbi Samuel Raphael. Rabbi Raphael had a strenuous time during the continuance of the war between the states, but through his fine executive ability and enthusiastic zeal he managed to keep his congregation together and the return of peace found it stronger than ever. Rabbi Raphael was a profound scholar, an eloquent speaker and a man of great personal magnetism. No man, Jew or Gentile, has ever stood higher in this community than he.

It was five years after the close of the war before an effort was made to secure a suitable house of worship by this congregation. In 1869 a building committee was appointed and in 1870, the cornerstone was laid for the first Synagogue, which was located on Franklin Avenue. Two sons of Rabbi Raphael, Benjamin and Mose, were prominent in the work of building this first house of worship for the congregation their father had done so much for spiritually.

The cornerstone for the Young Men's Christian Association was laid October 17, 1907, and the building was formally opened June 21, 1908. The building is one of the finest in the city.

Though it is said the first Christians in Houston were forced to hold religious services under the wide-spreading branches of a tree that grew on Market Square, their descendants are better provided for and today, by actual count, there are sixty-six houses of worship in this city, representing all shades of faith and belief. Houston is rapidly becoming a city of churches. Following is a list of the churches and chapels:

Methodist

Epworth Methodist Church; Harrisburg Methodist Episcopal Church; Grace Church, Houston Heights; McKee St. Methodist Church; First Methodist Church; Trinity Methodist Church; Bering Memorial Church; Washington Avenue Methodist Church; First Methodist Church of Houston Heights; McAshan Methodist; St. Paul's Methodist Church; Tabernacle Methodist Church; Brunner Avenue Methodist Church and Ebernezer German Methodist Church.

Presbyterian

First Presbyterian Church; First Presbyterian Church of Houston Heights; Hardy Street Presbyterian Church; Woodland Heights Presbyterian Church; Third Presbyterian Church; Oak Lawn Presbyterian Church; Second Presbyterian Church; Central Presbyterian Church; Westminister Presbyterian Church; Park Street Chapel; Market Street Chapel; Hutchins Street Chapel; Hyde Park Chapel and Blodgett Mission.

Episcopal

Christ Church; St. Mary's Episcopal Church; Trinity Church; St. John's Church and Clemens Memorial Church.

Baptist

First Baptist Church; Lee Avenue Baptist Church; Magnolia Baptist Church; Brunner Baptist Church; Calvary Baptist Church; Tabernacle Baptist Church; Emanuel Baptist Church; Bishop Street Baptist Church; Tuam Avenue Baptist Church ans Liberty Avenue Baptist Church.

Catholic

Church of the Annunciation; Sacred Heart Church; St. Joseph's Church; Church of the Blessed Sacrament and St. Patrick's Church.

Christian Church

Houston Heights Christian Church; Central Christian Church; Second Christian Church.

Apostolic Faith

Clark Street Mission; Brunner Tabernacle.

Lutheran

Trinity Evangelical Lutheran Church and First German Evangelical Lutheran Church.

Christian Science

First Church of Christ Scientist.

Congregational

First Congregational Church.

Evangelical Association

The Oak Lawn Church.

Church of Christ

First Church of Christ.

Spiritualist

The Spiritualists have a large society in Houston and hold regular meetings every Sunday.

The founding of Houston closely followed the Texas revolution, so it is not surprising to learn that there was a strong martial spirit among its citizens and that they should be willing and eager to embark in military movements that included active or prospectively active service. Governor Lubbock mentions in his memoirs that there were two military companies in Houston in the very early days. One of these, to which he belonged, saw service against the Indians, but there is nothing to show that the other had active service. These companies were what would be called state troops today.

In the early fifties there were two military companies here. One was the Washington Light Guards which held at that time very much the same place that the Houston Light Guard holds today. The other was the Milam Rifles organized after the Washington Light Guards had been in service for some time, and organized for the purpose of taking away from the Washington Light Guards the honors they had won, which were principally the smiles and admiration of the ladies. The two companies were about socially equal and there was intense rivalry between them, which occasionally led to personal collisions between the individual members.

On one occasion, during a target contest between the two companies on San Jacinto Day, there came near being something of a general riot because a lieutenant of one company and a private of the other went to war on their own account over a disputed score.

When the war broke out, instead of entering the Confederate Army as organizations, these two companies disbanded and the individual members joined new companies that were organized. The great bulk of the members of the Washington Light Guards joined the Bayou City Guards which afterwards earned such glory in the Army of Northern Virginia under Lee, known officially as Company A, 5th Texas Regiment, Hood's Brigade. In fact so many of the old company joined the Bayou City Guards that it was practically the old company itself.

Other members of both companies joined a cavalry company raised by the late Major Ike Stafford for service on the Rio Grande, which was the very first company to leave for the front at the breaking out of the war.

The Captain of the Washington Light Guards, Captain Edwards, raised still another company of infantry, while Captain Ed Riordan took some of the members of the Milam Rifles and with them as a nucleus formed a splendid company of infantry. It is doubtful if there was a single member of either of the two original companies who did not volunteer in some of the companies that left Houston in 1861.

At that time there was a boys' military company here, something on the order of the High School Cadets of today. This company was commanded by Captain W. M. Stafford, now of Galveston. When the war broke out, Captain Stafford and most of the older boys entered the Confederate Army. Captain Stafford was made a lieutenant in an artillery company and rose soon after to the rank of captain. He was, perhaps, the youngest captain in command of a battery in the Confederate service.

Another company that distinguished itself during the war was the Houston Turners, composed almost, if not entirely, of members of the Turnverein association. This company was organized and commanded by Captain E. B. H. Schneider and saw much active service, giving a good account of itself on several bloody fields.

The Confederate Grays was a fine infantry company from Houston that saw much active service, first at Shiloh under Johnston and afterwards in the campaign in Mississippi and at Vicksburg. After the capture of Vicksburg they were exchanged and transferred to this side of the river.

When the war began, it was looked on as a joke and there was much joking at the enthusiastic eagerness of the young men to get to the front. The Bayou City Guards was christened "The kid glove gentry," and when the company was ordered to Camp Van Dorn, below Harrisburg, for the purpose of being mustered into the service, preparatory to going to Virginia, Mr. T. W. House, Sr., sent them a big box of white kid gloves. The members put them on their bayonets and marched up Main Street with them thus displayed. Afterwards when the accomplishments of this company in the Army of Northern Virginia began to be known and bragged about, Mr. House was very proud of the "Kid glove gentry," and told frequently of how he had fitted them out for war with kid gloves.

After four years of actual warfare there was not much martial spirit left in the young men who returned home after the surrender. Consequently, there was no talk of organizing a company of play soldiers and the average returned veteran would shy at the sight of a sword or musket. However, there was a new crop of young men coming to the front and in 1873 some of these got together and organized the Houston Light Guard, a military company destined to shed as much honor and fame on Houston during peace times as the others had done during war.

The Houston Light Guard was organized April 21, 1873. Captain Fairfax Gray, a member of the United States Navy before the war and a distinguished officer in the Confederate Army, was the first captain of the company. For some reason the members soon lost interest and the organization practically ceased to exist. After the first meeting, none were held until late in the fall of the same year, when some of the most zealous of the young men got together and determined to reorganize the company.

This they did, electing J. R. Coffin captain. From that meeting dates the success of the Light Guard. Captain Coffin began regular drills and soon had the company in such form as to make a creditable showing as soldiers. The boys purchased uniforms, which were Confederate gray, and appeared in them for the first time in the great carnival of King Comus in February, 1874.

Four months later, when the May Volksfest was held, the Light Guard entered their first competitive drill, meeting four companies from outside points. Entering was all they did for they got no prize, but did get experience. The next year under Captain Joe Rice they won their first prize at the Austin drill, a sword valued at $500.

About that time there seems to have been a general revival of the martial spirit throughout the country and each city strove to secure a crack military company. All over the South and in many of the Northern and Western cities military companies were formed. While there was lots of pleasure and sport in indulging in this fad, it was very expensive and the heaviest expense fell on the individual members. Each company paid for its own travel expenses, its uniforms and everything, except its guns which were furnished by the State government. Interstate drills became all the rage and in 1881 the Houston Light Guard entered its first one at New Orleans where it competed against some of the crack companies of the South. The Light Guard took fourth prize, $500.

Their next appearance was in 1882 at the interstate drill that was held at Nashville, Tenn. There were five companies competing and the Light Guard took fourth prize again. However, they had the satisfaction of beating the Lawrence Rifles, a company that had come all the way from Boston, Mass. Beating that Boston company gave them the only bit of satisfaction they had.

However, the Light Guard were as strong in defeat as they afterwards proved themselves to be in the hour of victory. Captain Thomas Scurry was their commander and he determined to make them world-beaters, and did so before he completed his work. In the face of two or more failures they became more determined than ever and they were loyally backed by the businessmen of Houston.

In 1884 the businessmen raised a large sum of money to be used as prizes and to pay other expenses, and issued invitations to all the military companies in the United States to come to Houston for a great interstate drill. A number of crack companies promptly accepted the invitation. The War Department at Washington appointed three army officers to attend the drill, act as judges and make a report of results to the Department. Mr. H. Baldwin Rice was appointed manager of the drill, which took place at the Fairgrounds, where now stands the Fairgrounds Addition. The drill lasted a week. The first prize was $5,000. From that sum the prizes were reduced so that the last prize was only about one-quarter of that amount.

There was a state as well as an interstate drill held at the same time. In the interstate drill were such companies as the Treadway Rifles of St. Louis; the Columbus Guards of Columbus, Ga.; the Montgomery Greys of Montgomery, Ala.; the Washington Guards of Galveston, and the Houston Light Guard. The Houston Light Guard put up one of the most perfect drills that had ever been witnessed. They took first prize easily, as the following report of the army officers who were judges shows. The totals were as follows:

Houston Light Guard, 2.66; Treadway Rifles, 2.55; Columbus Guards, 2.35; Mobile Rifles, 2.29; Montgomery Greys, 2.28; Washington Guards, 1.95. A perfect drill would have given 3.00, the maximum score. To show how perfectly the Light Guard drilled, the following extract from the report of the judges is given:

> *Houston Light Guard*—It is observed that the inspection was nearly perfect. The appearance of the men in their dress, arms and accoutrements and their neatness, exceeded anything we have seen anywhere—each man like a color man at the United States Military Academy at West Point. Captain Scurry had not proceeded far in the programme when, while wheeling his company from column of twos, improperly, the company was placed in a position

from which it was almost impossible to extricate it, except as done, exhibiting great presence of mind on the captain's part. Captain Scurry's appreciation of the programme and its requirements was superior to that of the other commanders.

The ground was laid out with the view to testing the length and cadence of the step in quick and double time. A company marching as contemplated in the method applied would take the following number of steps in quick and double time, and in the time specified. In quick time, 284 steps in 2 minutes and 35 seconds; in double time, 284 steps in one minute and 26 seconds. The Houston Light Guard made the following record: In quick time, 283 steps in 2 minutes and 35 seconds; in double time, 1 minute and 27. Aside from all practice in this particular, the result was almost phenomenal. Captain Scurry was the only one who marched upon the flag with guide to the left as directed by the judges.

The Houston Light Guard generously offered to turn over the $5,000 first prize to the visiting companies to help pay their expenses, but the offer was refused with thanks, of course.

During 1885 the Houston Light Guard, under the able leadership of Captain Scurry, won three first prizes in interstate contests. These footed up $12,000. The first was at Mobile, Alabama, in May and the second a few days later in New Orleans. The third was in Philadelphia in July at the great drill that was held in Fairmount Park. In this drill and encampment nearly every section of the country was represented. There were seventy-five companies there, about one-half of them entering the interstate contest. The Houston Light Guard was an easy winner, the judges stating that there was enough room between their score and that of their nearest competitor to place three or four companies.

From Philadelphia the company went to New York, where they were royally entertained by the famous New York regiments. It is only an act of justice to give here the names of the officers and men who made the Houston Light Guard "world-beaters." They were:

Captain, Thos. Scurry;
1st Lieutenant, F. A. Reichardt;
2nd Lieutenant, T. H. Franklin;
3rd Lieutenant, Spencer Hutchins;

Quartermaster, W. A. Childress;
Surgeon, Dr. S. O. Young;
1st Sergeant, George L. Price;
2nd Sergeant, R. A. Scurry;
1st Corporal, H. D. Taylor;
2nd Corporal, W. K. Mendenhall;
3rd Corporal, George N. Torrey.

Privates—Byers, Barnett, Bates, Bull, Byres, Cook, Dealy, Foss, Golihart, Hodgson, Hutchins, Heyer, Reynaud, Swanson, Johnson, Journey, Wilson, R. Kattman, E. Kattman, Lewis, Mahoney, Mitchell, McKeever, Powell, Randolph, Steel, Sawyer, Sharpe, Tyler, Taft, Taylor, Torrey, Wisby. Perpetual drummer, John Sessums (colored).

The next great victory of the Light Guard was at Galveston in 1886, where they took the first prize, a purse of $4,500, in competition with such companies as the Montgomery True Blues, San Antonio Rifles, Branch Guards of St. Louis, Company F, Louisville Legion and Belknap Rifles of San Antonio. That drill of the Light Guard was the most perfect ever witnessed in the United States and excited widespread wonder and admiration among military men and the general public.

The Light Guard went to Austin in 1888 and took first prize, $5,000, in competition with some of the crack companies in the U.S. The next year Galveston had another great interstate drill and, in order to not bluff off other companies, the Galveston people barred the Houston Light Guard, thus paying them the highest compliment they ever received. Galveston gave the Light Guard a special prize of $500 for an exhibition drill.

The Houston Light Guard showed that they were not merely fancy soldiers when the war with Spain began. They volunteered promptly and, under command of Captain George McCormick, went to the front. They saw service in Florida and Cuba. When peace negotiations began, Captain McCormick returned home and R. A. Scurry became captain of the company, returning home with it soon after. The Light Guard owns its armory, the handsomest in the state. It was paid for partly with money won as prizes and partly by issuing bonds. The property, in the business section of the city, has become extremely valuable and could be disposed of today at many times its cost to the company.

The following are the captains who have commanded the Houston Light Guard from its organization to the present day: Fairfax Gray, John Coffin, Joe S. Rice, George Price, James S. Baker, Jr., Thomas Scurry, F. A. Reichardt, George McCormick, R. A. Scurry, C. Hutchinson, Milby Porter and Dallas J. Mathews, the present able captain.

Troop A has always been the crack troop of cavalry of the Texas National Guards. This is a Houston company and during the war with Spain was part of the First Texas Cavalry, United States Volunteers.

The Jeff Miller Rifles, which belonged to the Second Infantry regiment, was also a noted company, that saw service during the skirmish with Spain.

CHAPTER IX:
MADE IN HOUSTON

While there was quite a large sawmill, a gristmill, blacksmith shop and lumberyard at Harrisburg, established there by Mr. Robert Wilson, father of the late Mr. Jas. T. D. Wilson, who came to Texas in 1828, it would not be exactly fair to claim these as the first Houston manufacturing enterprises. The first strictly Houston concern in the manufacturing line, if a sawmill falls under that head, was the old sawmill that stood just about where the Milam Street bridge crosses Buffalo Bayou. That mill was built in the early forties.

Mr. Elim Stockbridge built a cornmeal mill at the foot of Texas Avenue in 1844. The *Morning Star* was greatly pleased with this evidence of progress and gave quite a glowing account of the motive power which was three oxen on a treadmill.

During the same year Mr. N. T. Davis erected the first compress in Houston. The *Morning Star*, speaking of this compress in its issue of March 11, 1844, says:

> A few days ago we visited the cotton compress lately erected in this city by Mr. N. T. Davis, and were agreeably surprised to find that the machine used for compressing cotton bales admirably answers the purposes for which it was constructed. With the aid of only two hands, Mr. Davis can compress a bale of 500 pounds into a space only 22 inches square in 15 minutes. The facility with which the work is done is truly surprising.

Since the best modern compress can turn out a 500-pound bale compressed into a space of 22 cubic feet, it is evident that the editor of the *Star* got his notes mixed when he wrote of "22 square inches."

In 1845 there was a rope-walk on the block now owned by the Houston Turnverein. It was used for manufacturing rope until about 1853 or 54. The first iron foundry was established in Houston in 1851 by Mr. Alex McGowan on the north side of Buffalo Bayou and on the banks of White Oak Bayou. For the first year or two its principal work was in making kettles for the sugar plantations near here and in constructing light machinery for farm and plantation use. However, after the Houston & Texas Central road began operation, the work of the foundry increased and it was kept busy doing repair work for the road. For several years this foundry was the largest and best in Texas and did an immense amount of all kinds of foundry work. Even during the war it was enabled to continue a regular foundry business, something that others were not able or willing to do.

About 1858 or 59, one of the best and most expert foundrymen in the business came here from the North. This was Mr. Cushman, the owner and manager of Cushman's Foundry, which was located on the south side of the west end of Preston Avenue bridge. Mr. Cushman put up extensive buildings and established suitable machinery for doing all kinds of pattern-making and foundry work. About the time he got everything going smoothly, the war came on and as his workmen volunteered almost to a man, in the Confederate Army. He was left with an expensive plant on his hands and no labor to use it. He struggled along in a haphazard way for awhile and then converted his plant into an arsenal and began manufacturing cannon, shells and such things for the Confederate government. The commander of this department detailed skilled mechanics to do the work and, before long, Cushman's Foundry became one of the most important concerns in the State. After the war Mr. Cushman restored his plant to its original use and did a large foundry business for many years, finally disposing of the plant.

Perhaps the most successful manufacturing enterprise to grow from an insignificant beginning is the Dickson Car Wheel Works. When Mr. Dickson first announced that he was going to manufacture car wheels here he was laughed at and certain defeat was predicted. He persisted, however, and today the Dickson Car Wheel Works are among the largest and most profitable establishments of that character in the South. There is a steady and constantly growing demand for their output.

The first artificial ice made in Houston was at a plant established by Dr. Pearl, who was associated with two young Englishmen. These gentlemen established an ice-making plant and also a meat packery on the Bayou below the city in 1869. Lack of experience, being rather in advance of the times and other causes combined to frustrate their designs and after a year or two of hopeless struggle the plant proved a failure and went out of business in 1873.

During 1875, Mr. E. W. Taylor and one or two associates bought some of the abandoned machinery of the Pearl plant and established a regular packery. The next year Mr. Geiselman established another packery, and both of them did a good business for some years. Transportation facilities were unsatisfactory and that limited the field of operation of the two plants to such an extent that both voluntarily went out of business. Not until 1894 did Houston come to the front as a packing house center. That year the Houston Packing Company's plant was established here. This is the largest independent packing house in the United States and does a business of about $4,000,000 annually.

Both the Swift and Armour companies maintain branches here and own their own buildings. Every large packing house in the United States has a branch office or agency in Houston, induced to come here by Houston's admirable facilities for receiving and distributing their products.

Since the packing house part of the old Pearl plant was, in a measure, resurrected through the efforts of Mr. Taylor and his associates, one would have supposed that attention would have been given to ice-making also. That was not true, however, for it was not until 1880 that a successful ice manufacturing plant was established. That was the Central Ice Company, organized by Mr. Hugh Hamilton. The first machinery was a dilapidated and abandoned ice machine. This is today one of the largest and most successful plants in the state. The American Brewing Company is another large and flourishing concern. It was chartered in 1894 and its principal owner is Mr. A. Busch of St. Louis.

Today Houston has a number of large ice-making plants. Chief among them are the Houston Packing Company, the Henke Artesian Ice and Refrigerating Company, the Crystal Ice and Fuel Company and the Irvin Ice Factory.

Shortly after the close of the war, one or two attempts were made to establish cotton mills here. Not until 1872 was the movement successful. In that year the City Cotton Mills were erected in the Second Ward. Mr. B. A. Shepherd was the principal stockholder, owning slightly more than half of the stock. The mill was just beginning to do a good business, when, in August, 1875, it was destroyed by fire. The loss was complete, being $200,000, with no insurance.

A few years later Mr. E. H. Cushing and Mr. James F. Dumble started another cotton mill out at Eureka, five miles from Houston on the Houston & Texas Central Railroad, but after a struggling existence of a year or two, they were forced to abandon the undertaking.

From that time until 1903 no further attempt was made to build cotton or textile mills here. However, in 1903, the Oriental Textile Mills were established, and this institution now ranks among the largest and most successful textile mills in the United States.

At the close of the war there were several small wagon and vehicle manufacturing concerns established here, and there were also one or two planing mills and sash factories. The planing mills and sash factories of Bering & Cortes and of Henry House were the principal ones, and both did an immense business. As remarked, the manufacture of wagons, while one of the earliest of Houston's manufacturing enterprises, was never carried on extensively until a year or two ago, when in 1910, the Eller Wagon Works were established here. This concern does an immense business and manufactures heavy trucks, oil-tank wagons and such things, which are distributed over the state.

Aside from having several skillful cabinetmakers who did fine but limited work, no attention was paid to the manufacture of furniture on a large scale until in 1904, when the Myers-Spalti Company established their plant here. This is one of the largest and most prosperous plants of its kind in the country. The firm makes anything and everything in the way of furniture. They employ only the best and most expert workmen. They have branch offices in all the leading markets, and the amount of their business is immense.

A fact not generally known is that Houston has the only piano and organ manufacturing plant in the South. It was established here in 1909 and is now doing a good and lucrative business. The work turned out by them beings of the highest order of excellence.

Houston's standing and importance in the nation as a manufacturing point is demonstrated by the U.S. Census Report. Following are the figures for Houston, for 1909, the year when the figures were taken by the government:

Number of establishments, 249; capital invested, $16,594,000; cost of material used, $14,321,000; salaries and wages, $4,254,000; miscellaneous expenses, $1,942,000; value of products, $23,016,000; value added by manufacture, $8,695,000; number of salaried officers and clerks, 725; average number of wage earners, 5338; total number of steam laundries, 9; capital invested in laundries, $270,000; cost of material used, $74,000; salaries and wages, $256,000; miscellaneous expenses, $129,000; value of products, $500,000; number of salaried officers and clerks, 34; average number of wage earners, 422.

When the government figures were taken in 1909, comparison was made with those of 1904 to show percentage of increase and decrease. The comparisons for Houston are as follows:

Increase in cost of material used, 88 per cent; increase in capital invested, 87 per cent; increase in number of salaried officers and clerks, 75 per cent; increase in miscellaneous expenses, 72 per cent; increase in value of products, 70 per cent; increase in value added by manufacture, 46 per cent; increase in salaries and wages, 24 per cent; increase in number of establishments, 19 per cent; increase in average number of wage earners employed during the year, 6 per cent.

In many ways Houston is an ideal point for manufacturing enterprises. An inexhaustible supply of the purest artesian water can be obtained anywhere in or for miles around the city, while the question of fuel is almost as easily solved, since Houston is just on the edge of the great oil field and is connected by pipelines with all the fields as far north as Oklahoma. Water can be had at the small cost of sinking a well, while there is an abundance of the best and cheapest fuel. When to these advantages is added the superb transportation facilities possessed by Houston, it is surprising that there are not a hundred-fold more great manufacturing enterprises here than there are.

Perhaps no city in the United States had among its early settlers so many
prominent and distinguished men as had Houston. As a rule, new cities as
well as new countries are settled by pioneers who are distinguished more
for their brawn and muscle than for their culture and intelligence. Hard
work, requiring strength and endurance, counts for more in a new country
than courtly manners and scientific ability. These latter belong rather to
the children of pioneers than to the pioneers themselves. Houston affords a
striking exception to this rule, for among her early settlers were some of the
greatest, most prominent and intellectual men in America. This was as true
of the foreign element as of the native-born Americans. In fact the latter,
as a whole, contrasted rather unfavorably with the distinguished Germans
who were among the first settlers. While the Americans excelled naturally
in statecraft and in the legal and medical professions, being far more ac-
customed to the needs, requirements and customs of this country than their
foreign friends and associates, the latter contributed more largely to the
arts, sciences and general literature. Thus, between the two, Houston was
placed on a most advantageous plane at the very beginning.

It must not be supposed that the learned professions, the arts or anything
that related to literature occupied the stage to the exclusion of everything
else, for that was far from true. There were lots of typical pioneers, rough
men, but all men; and in addition to these there were typical "bad men"
and toughs. These latter were in a woeful minority and were too few and
insignificant to stamp their individuality on the community.

While Houston and Galveston have always been strong business rivals
and have never failed to give each other commercial black eyes when opportunity presented, the people of both cities have always been the best of
friends in a social way and have done much good for each other. The first
literary society, lyceum or whatever it was called, in Texas was located in
Galveston in the early forties. While nominally a Galveston institution,
this society was loyally supported by Houstonians who contributed regularly to the monthly entertainments that were given.

In 1848 the Houston Lyceum was chartered. Almost before it was born,
it went to sleep and did not wake until 1854. That year it was revived and
showed considerable animation for awhile but soon lapsed into innocuous

desuetude. At that time 382 volumes had been gotten together and a bookcase had been purchased.

For a short time considerable interest was taken in the affairs of the Lyceum by the gentlemen having its management in hand, but they soon grew weary and the Lyceum was allowed to die again. During the war nothing was, or could be, done, but at the close of the war an attempt was made to revive interest in it. This effort met with only partial success. Spasmodic attempts were made to establish the Lyceum firmly on its feet, but it was not until 1895 that such an attempt was crowned with success.

In that year Mrs. Looscan, president of the Ladies Reading Club, brought that Club to the assistance of the Lyceum. Every member of the Club became a member of the Lyceum and the books were removed to a room in the Mason building. Through the efforts of these ladies, the city officials were induced to give official recognition to the Lyceum in 1899 and to make an appropriation of $200 monthly for its support.

The next year Mr. Carnegie gave $50,000 for a library building fund, providing the city would donate a suitable building site. The conditions were complied with and the present library building was formally opened to the public in March, 1904. In 1900 the Houston Lyceum and Carnegie Association was chartered and took the place of the old Houston Lyceum. About the same time Mr. N. S. Meldrum endowed the children's department with $6,000 as a memorial to Norma Meldrum.

Miss Julia Ideson, the librarian, stated in her report for 1904 that there had been 59,751 books withdrawn from the library for home use. At that time there were between eight and nine thousand volumes in the library. In her report for the municipal year ending February 29, 1912, Miss Ideson says, "The circulation from the main library amounted to 102,580 volumes, an increase of more than 8,000 volumes over the circulation of last year. In addition to the above 5,177 books have been distributed through the other distributing agencies." On May 1, 1911, there were 31,678 volumes in the library. During the year that just closed there was a net gain of 3,657 volumes bringing the total number of volumes in the library May 1, 1912, to 35,426.

The officers of the Houston Lyceum and Carnegie Library Association are: Mr. E. L. Dennis, president; Mrs. H. F. Ring, vice-president; Mrs. I. S. Meyer, secretary; Mrs. E. N. Gray, treasurer; Mrs. E. Raphael, corresponding secretary, and Miss Julia Ideson, librarian.

The Ladies Reading Club, organized in 1885 by Mrs. M. Looscan and Mrs. C. M. Lombardi, is the oldest and largest of Houston's purely literary clubs. The Ladies Shakespeare Club was organized in 1890 with Mesdames E. Raphael, I. G. Gerson, I. Blandin, Blanche Booker and Misses C. R. Redwood, Lydia Adkisson and Mary Light as charter members. This club has kept its organization and has been in active existence since its formation. Another Shakespeare Club was organized in 1904 by Mrs. A. G. Howell, Mrs. J. W. Lockett and Mrs. J. W. Carter. This club is very active and great interest is taken by its members in the work they have outlined for themselves.

Perhaps the most interesting of the women's clubs in Houston is the Current Literature Club, which was organized in 1899 by Mrs. Si Packard. The club was originally organized for the purpose of reading current novels and light literature, but members soon grew ambitious and more substantial books were taken up and discussed, until today the club represents through its members the cultured literary taste of Houston.

The Houston Pen Womens' Association was organized in 1906 by eighteen ladies who met at the residence of Mrs. William Christian for the purpose of forming an association composed of ladies engaged in newspaper and literary work. Mrs. Elizabeth Strong Tracy was chosen as the first president and Mrs. Dancey as first secretary. The membership consists of historians, poets, authors, journalists and newspaper workers. The association has been wonderfully successful, showing a consistent growth and influence ever since the day of its organization.

A Chapter of the Daughters of the American Revolution was organized in Houston in 1899 by Mrs. Seabrook W. Sydnor, who had been appointed regent by the general organization. The chapter took the name of Lady Washington Chapter. The organization has been in active operation since its organization and has accomplished a great deal in the way of patriotic work.

San Jacinto Chapter No. 2, Daughters of the Republic of Texas, was organized in 1901. The chapter has accomplished a wonderful amount of valuable work, in perpetuating the memory of those who fought for Texas' independence, and has collected valuable historical data. This chapter has taken under its care San Jacinto battlefield and has marked with suitable monuments and tablets, historical points and localities associated with early Texas history.

Robert E. Lee Chapter, 186, United Daughters of the Confederacy, was organized in 1897 and Oran M. Roberts Chapter, 440, United Daughters of the Confederacy, was organized in 1901. Each chapter has a large membership and their meetings are always largely attended. Since their organization they have accomplished much good, both in the way of collecting and preserving historical data and in looking after indigent and disabled Confederate veterans.

There are a great many charitable, musical and literary associations in Houston, nearly every one organized and kept alive by the ladies. Nearly all the societies, in the beginning, had meeting places of their own, but since the completion of the Library building nearly all of them meet in the elegant quarters provided for that purpose by the Library Association.

The Labor associations of Houston are numerous and thoroughly organized. The following facts are taken from a statement published by Mr.
Max Andrew, editor of the Labor Journal:

The total number of industrial workers in Houston is 25,000, graded
as follows: Men, 15,000; women, 6,000; children fifteen years and under,
4,000. Organized: Men, 55 per cent; women, 2 per cent. Of the skilled
trades, 85 per cent are organized and 15 per cent unorganized.

During the last ten years the hours of labor have been decreased, all along
the line, from ten hours to eight hours. During the last ten years there has
been an average increase in wages of 25 per cent. However, against that increase is placed the increased cost of living which amounts to 40 per cent.

The total number of organized men and women in Houston is 8,250. The
plumbers, printers, brickmasons, plasterers, stonecutters and marble cut-
ters are the best organized of any of the crafts. All trades limit the number
of apprentices. This has done much towards maintaining a living wage for
the journeyman. Public sentiment and feeling towards union labor in this
city and community is very favorable and all important work is done by
union labor.

Since the general public has only a vague idea of labor matters and of
the conditions that prevail in labor circles, the following extracts are taken
from Mr. Andrew's article, as matters of useful information. The following
are the working conditions that prevail in various branches of labor, both
organized and unorganized:

In the packing houses 500 men, women and children are employed.
Wages, for men, $1.50 to $2.00 per day; for women, 75 cents to $2.00 per
day; for children, 50 cents to $1.00 per day. No Sunday work. Little oppor-
tunity for training or educational advancement. Employees not organized.

In the railroad shops and yards, there are about 4,000 employed. About
25 per cent of laborers work on Sundays. Conditions very good for training
and educational advancement. Average wage for all employees about $2.50
per day. Ninety per cent of workers organized.

In the cotton-oil mills and compresses there are about 1,500 employed.
Wages of men, $1.50 to $2.50 per day; women, $1.00 to $1.25 per day;
children, 50 cents to 75 cents per day. Work covers only six months of the

year. No opportunity for training or educational advancement. Conditions are far in advance of those found in other Southern States.

In the sawmills and factories the number of employees is 500. Wages for skilled men, $2.50 to $3.00 per day; unskilled men, 75 cents to $1.75 per day; women, 50 cents to $1.00 per day; children, 25 cents to 75 cents per day. Little opportunity for training or educational advancement. About 10 per cent organized.

In the general stores there are about 3,000 employed. Wages for men, $5.00 to $18.00 per week; women, $3.50 to $10 per week; children, $1.50 to $5.00 per week. Conditions are deplorable. Not one in a thousand of the employees has the slightest chance for training or educational advancement. Unless the general public interferes, Houston will soon parallel the large cities where young womanhood is sacrificed at the altar of greed and avarice. This labor is unorganized.

There are about 500 employed at the breweries. Working conditions are exceptionably good. Wages range from $2.00 to $5.00 per day; hours of labor, eight per day. The breweries operate 24 hours per day, labor being divided into three shifts of eight hours each. Employees thoroughly organized. All workmen in the breweries, where steadily employed, must join the Brewers Union.

There are about 5,000 common laborers in Houston. Wages, for men $1.25 to $2.00 per day; women, 50 cents to $1.25 per day; children, 25 cents to $1.00 per day. Only about 10 per cent of these laborers are organized.

There are about 3,000 employed in the industrial crafts. That is in addition to those working in railroad shops, mills, etc.

Carpenters and Joiners—Approximately 75% organized. Wages, union, $4.00 per day; non-union, $3.50 per day. Educational and training conditions are fine. No Sunday work. Steady employment the entire year round.

Plasterers—Conditions are good. 90 per cent organized. Wages, for union men, $6.00 per day; for non-union men, $3.50 per day. No Sunday work.

Sheetmetal Workers—Steady work the whole year. Wages, union men, $3.50 to $4.50 per day. Non-union men, lower. About 90 per cent of the craft organized.

Brickmasons—Conditions are fine. Wages, union men, $6.00 to $7.00 per day; non-union men, $3.00 to $4.00 per day. About 95 per cent organized.

Machinists—Steady work all the year. Wages, union men, $3.80 per day; non-union men, $2.50 per day.

Theatrical Stage Employees—Conditions reasonably good. Wages range from $15.00 to $25.00 per week. Every day work, including Sunday.

Blacksmiths—About 65 per cent organized. Wages, union men, $3.80 per day; non-union men, $2.50 per day.

Lathers—Steady employment. Wages, union men, $4.00 to $6.00 per day; non-union men, $2.50 per day.

Printers—Thoroughly organized. Wages, $3.50 to $8.00 per day, according to men and position. About 75 per cent of printers are homeowners.

Pressmen—Thoroughly organized. Wages, $3.50 per day. There are also many homeowners among the pressmen.

Bookbinders—Thoroughly organized. Work eight hours per day. Wages, $4.00 per day.

Electrical Workers—About 80 per cent organized. Wages, $3.50 to $4.50 per day. All members at work.

Bartenders—About 80 per cent organized. Wages $15.00 to $21.00 per week.

Tailors—Poorly organized. Hours of labor, ten hours per day. Wages, $2.00 to $3.00 per day, mostly in piece work.

Coopers—Thoroughly organized. Average wages, $2.85 to $4.00 per day. Hours of labor, eight hours per day.

Bridge and Structural Iron Workers—Organized 100 per cent. Hours of labor, eight. Wages, $3.50 to $4.50 per day. Plenty of work. Duties most hazardous.

Boiler makers—About 90 per cent organized. Wages, $3.50 to $5.00 per day for union men; non-union men, scale lower.

Marble Workers—Thoroughly organized. Wages, $4.00 to $6.00 per day. Work eight hours a day.

Journeyman Barbers—Both white and negroes organized. Conditions above the average. No Sunday work.

Elevator Constructors—Thoroughly organized. All employed at present. No Sunday work. Wages $4.00 per day.

Pattern Makers—Well organized. Work nine hours a day. Wages 50 cents per hour.

Garment Workers—This is the only organized craft of women workers. Membership about 200 strong. Work, eight hours a day. Wages, $9.00

to $18.00 per week. No Sunday labor. Sanitary conditions exceptionally good.

Horseshoers—Organized about 75 per cent. Wages, $2.50 to $3.50 per day. Work eight hours a day.

Stationary Engineers—Organized about 80%. Average wages about $3.00 to $4.00 per day.

Painters, Decorators and Paperhangers—Organized about 80 per cent. Work eight hours per day. Wages, $3.50 to $4.00 per day.

Plumbers—Thoroughly organized. Work eight hours a day. Wages $6.00. The union has many educational features to perfect the skill of its members.

CHAPTER XII:
COMMERCE, COTTON, RICE AND TIMBER

Unquestionably the first commercial organization in Texas was the old Chamber of Commerce organized in Houston April 5, 1840, with Mr. Perkins as president. Unfortunately this association has left nothing but a name, for there is no record of work done by it, though it is fair to presume that it accomplished some of the objects for which it was formed.

Not for thirty-four years was another attempt made to form a commercial body in this city. On May 16, 1874, a number of the prominent businessmen of Houston met in one of the parlors of the Hutchins House and organized the Houston Board of Trade and Cotton Exchange. Mr. C. S. Longcope was elected president, Mr. Wm. J. Hutchins, vice-president and Mr. George W. Kidd, secretary.

The new organization went actively to work. Perkins Hall, used also as a theatre at times, was leased. Mr. Kidd purchased some small blackboards and with no other furniture or fixings, the Exchange was officially declared open and ready for business. At that time telegraph tolls were very high, in fact they were prohibitive so far as the new exchange was concerned. The amount of commercial news and quotations received by the exchange in a full working day was about equal to that now received in a few minutes, even on dull days. Mr. Kidd helped out the quotations by using the scant commercial report received by the *Houston Telegraph*, of which paper he was also commercial editor.

Conditions such as these prevailed for the first three years of the Exchange's existence, or until 1877. In that year businessmen appear to have recognized the great values of the Exchange and rallied to its support. Something like a reorganization took place within the Exchange. A new charter was obtained and the name of the organization was changed to the Houston Cotton Exchange and Board of Trade. New rules and regulations were adopted, the initiation fee was increased and provision was made for a regular and permanent income through fees and dues, for the support of the Exchange. From that moment the course of the exchange has been upward, until today no commercial body in the South stands higher in every way than the Houston Cotton Exchange and Board of Trade.

Not content with caring for the large and constantly growing cotton business of Houston, the Exchange was always found in the front ranks working for the good and advancement of the city. For a number of years the Exchange has had among its standing committees one whose special duty it is to look after the welfare of the ship channel. When the present Chamber of Commerce was formed, the Cotton Exchange turned over an immense amount of work to it that before that was tended to by the Exchange. It retained its interest in the ship channel, however, and while working in perfect harmony with the Chamber of Commerce and all other Houston organizations, it is still found working most zealously.

In 1883 the members of the Exchange determined to build a home of their own. Ground was purchased, plans adopted and on November 15, 1884, the new building was turned over to the Exchange by the contractors. It was a very handsome, though small, building and answered every purpose for which it had been constructed for many years. In later years it was remodeled. Additional stories were added and today the Exchange building is one of the most attractive and valuable buildings in the city.

There is no cotton exchange in the South more prosperous Houston's Exchange. When it was first organized a membership cost but $1 a month. A certificate of membership now costs $2,000 and is difficult to secure one at even that price. Annual dues on each certificate are $50, while provision is made for fees and other dues to maintain the exchange.

The following gentleman have served as president of the Exchange since its organization:

C. S. Longcope	1874-75	Wm. D. Cleveland	1884-91
Wm. D. Cleveland	1875-76	Wm. Read	1891-92
George L. Porter	1876-77	H. W. Garrow	1892-1902
H. R. Percy	1877-78	Wm. D. Cleveland	1902-05
S. K. McIlhenny	1878-79	W. E. Andrews	1905-06
Wm. V. R. Watson	1879-80	H. R. Percy	1877-78
A. H. Lea	1880-81	W. O. Ansley	1906-07
S. K. McIlhenny	1881-82	E. W. Taylor	1907-08
S. A. McAshan	1882-84	A. L. Nelms	1908-12

Mr. George W. Kidd, the first secretary of the Exchange, served actively until 1898 when he became secretary emeritus. He was succeeded by Mr. B. W. Martin who resigned to accept a more lucrative position and was succeeded in turn by Mr. B. R. Warner. Mr. Warner, after serving from

1899 to 1903, resigned to return to newspaper work in New Orleans. In 1904 Mr. W. J. DeTreville was elected secretary and served until June, 1910, when, on his death, Mr. J. F. Burwell, the present efficient secretary was elected.

With its immense lumber, oil, rice and manufacturing interests Houston long ago passed that point in its progress where its prosperity depended on any single commodity or industry. Like other commercial centers, Houston for some years counted heavily on its cotton receipts for its prosperity, but does so no longer. The modern Houston merchants are not indifferent to the great value of the cotton business, however. They are anxious to get all of it possible, and with the object of doing so, they have left nothing undone to make this the most attractive market and concentrating point in the South. They have constructed large compresses and cotton warehouses and now have some of the largest and most conveniently situated buildings of that kind on this continent.

The great fire which occurred in the Fifth Ward early this year destroyed three of Houston's fine compresses. There are three large ones left and two are being constructed on so great a scale that when completed in time to handle the coming crop, Houston will have the finest facilities for handling and caring for cotton in the South.

The presses destroyed were the Cleveland, the Standard and the Southern, their combined capacity of presses being 3,000 bales daily and their storage capacity about 100,000 bales. The Cleveland and the Merchants have combined and plans are now being perfected for the erection of the finest and largest compress and warehouse in the world. The storage capacity will be limited only by the restrictions of the insurance companies. They are unwilling to insure so great an amount of cotton as the company could care for. It is certain that the storage capacity of the new press will not be less than 300,000 bales. The company owns something like seventy acres of land on the ship channel and therefore will not be restricted by want of space. Captain W. D. Cleveland is the head of the new company.

Houston already has in the Magnolia Warehouse and Storage Company one of the best equipped, largest and most powerful presses in the country. Every compress and warehouse in Houston is located either on the banks of the bayou or on a railroad and all of them have rail connection. The result is that drayage, a costly feature in handling cotton, is entirely eliminated and the business is conducted economically and expeditiously. Last season there were shipped down the bayou about 400,000 bales of cotton. As each bale represented a saving to the owner of 12 1/2 cents because there was no drayage, it is evident that the shipments represented about $50,000 in savings. No other cotton market in the world can or does do business so cheaply.

The history of Houston's cotton business is of more than passing interest since in its entirety it represents every phase of the evolution of the world's cotton trade. As already noted in these pages, in the early days all cotton raised in the state was brought here by ox-wagons for marketing. The Houston merchants bought the cotton both with cash and groceries and goods. It was a most satisfactory method of doing business and both the farmer and merchant profited by the transaction. After the merchant had accumulated a sufficient number of bales to warrant it, he shipped the cotton down the bayou to Galveston to be placed on chartered vessels, to be shipped to Liverpool or other foreign markets. Since there was no way of knowing how prices were ruling in the foreign markets, the merchant guarded against possible loss by discounting his last information materially and paying from seven to ten dollars per bale less for the cotton than he estimated it to be worth. This was fair since there was always serious danger of a heavy decline in prices before the cotton could arrive on the other side.

After the railroads were built in Texas, Galveston became the great cotton market of the state and every bale raised in Texas was shipped there. One thing that helped build up Galveston was the fact that there were no such things as through bills of lading and rail rates favored the port. In 1874, J. H. Blake & Co. established their firm in Houston and soon evolved a plan for overcoming the disadvantages under which Houston was placed. By an arrangement made with the Houston & Texas Central and the International Railroads this firm was enabled to buy cotton in the interior, bring it to Houston and then ship it out again either by rail or by water. Under this arrangement Messrs. Blake & Co. made the first shipment of cotton from an interior point to a foreign market on a through bill of lading in 1874. This was the first shipment of the kind ever made. That method of doing business soon placed Houston, if not on an equal footing, at least on nearly such with Galveston and saved this market from utter extinction.

Then the system of buying and selling future contracts was established. This was perhaps the greatest advance that could possibly have been made towards stability of the cotton market, and the establishment of something like uniform prices all over the world. The system was very simple. Cotton was purchased on this side only when prices in Liverpool were favorable for such purchases. The cost of freight, insurance, commission and other charges were added to the price paid for the cotton and then, if Liverpool prices were sufficiently high to warrant doing so, the cotton was bought and future contracts sold in Liverpool by cable. In that way every possible chance of loss was eliminated from the transaction. When the cotton arrived on the other side the future contract was closed out; the difference in the price of the contract and the price of the actual cotton equaled each other.

The next great change that took place was more radical and far-reaching. In their effort to do away with middlemen, the spinners on the other side established buying agencies of their own on this side. These, in turn, established sub-agencies all over the country, so that the producer of cotton instead of having to seek a market, found one right at his door. There was such competition between the buyers that the highest prices possible were paid in order to get the cotton. Every crossroad and little town in the state became a center of information about prices and the farmer could learn every morning the quotation of that day both in American and foreign markets.

It soon became evident that it would be necessary to provide some place where large quantities of cotton could be concentrated for inspection, classification and arranging for final shipment. The Houston cotton men realized that a radical change in the method of marketing cotton was about to take place and they began at once to prepare themselves to care for this concentrated cotton. Old warehouses and compresses were enlarged and new ones erected. The storing capacity of the city was materially increased and when the work was finished, Houston was most thoroughly equipped to meet all demands that could be made on her.

Another thing that was done, which shows the great forethought of the Houston merchants, was reducing all local charges to the lowest point possible. No attempt was made to make money directly from the compresses and warehouses, as such, but these were used very much as so much capital, to attract and keep the cotton business here. It is a fact that cannot be disputed that today Houston's local charges on a bale of cotton are from 25 cents to 30 cents per bale cheaper than are those in any other cotton market in the South. Now when to this saving in local charges is added the further saving of from 10 cents to 12 cents through the absence of drayage, it is readily seen why so much cotton is shipped here and why Houston stands so prominently forward as a great cotton market.

Mention has been made of the Chamber of Commerce that was organized in Houston in 1840, but the present magnificent body of that name has no direct nor indirect connection with that early body. The Chamber of Commerce of today is for today and looks more to future accomplishments than to traditions of the past.

The immediate forerunner of the Chamber of Commerce was the Houston Business League, which was organized in 1895 by about forty gentlemen who sought to form an association that would look after the best interests of Houston. Col. R. M. Johnston, editor of the *Houston Post*, and Mr. W. W. Dexter, at present editor and proprietor of the *Bankers' Journal*, were prime movers in the organization and did much to insure its success. The constitution adopted declared the following to be the object of the association:

> The object of the Houston Business League is to promote immigration, to create and extend and foster the trade, commerce and manufacturing interests of Houston; to secure and build up transportation lines; to secure reasonable and equitable transportation rates; to build up and maintain the value of our real estate, progressive, efficient and economical administration of our municipal government, to collect, preserve and disseminate information in relation to our commercial, financial and industrial affairs and to unite, as far as possible, our people in one representative body.

The following gentlemen were chosen as the first officers of the new organization: J. M. Cotton, president; Ed Kiam, first vice president; J. C. Bering, second vice president; E. T. Heiner, third vice president; W. W. Dexter, secretary; Guy H. Harcourt, treasurer.

After serving for only a short time, Secretary Dexter resigned and Mr. George P. Brown was chosen as his successor. The election of Mr. Brown was a most fortunate thing for the Business League, since he brought to its service splendid executive and administrative talent and a wonderful amount of energy and zeal. Under Mr. Brown's administration the Business League forged rapidly to the front. A large number of manufacturing and industrial plants were secured for Houston, the Floral Festival and

No-Tsu-Oh associations were formed and the name of the city was placed permanently on the map of the country.

In 1910 the Business League was enlarged and a necessary reorganization took place. The name Business League was dropped and the organization became the Houston Chamber of Commerce. Mr. Adolph Boldt was secretary at the time and it was largely due to him that the scope of the association's objects and energy were enlarged. He recognized the magnitude of the field and the Chamber of Commerce was organized to fill every part of it.

In the Chamber of Commerce there is a general association, but all the details of practical work are in the hands of special committees who have absolute authority and freedom of action, being responsible only to the general association. These committees are called bureaus. There is, for instance, the Traffic Bureau, to which is referred all matters relating to freight rates, rate discriminations and questions of that kind. There is a Convention Bureau which looks after securing conventions to meet in Houston and looks after the entertainment of strangers who come to such conventions. There is a Publicity Bureau, an Industrial Bureau, which looks after securing manufacturing and industrial concerns for Houston, and a number of other important bureaus.

It is obvious how thoroughly organized the Chamber of Commerce is. One of the most pleasing features connected with the organization is the perfect harmony that exists between it and other organizations working either directly or indirectly towards accomplishing the same ends. The citizens attest their faith in the Chamber of Commerce by giving it the most loyal support, and it is today one of the strongest and most efficient organizations of its kind in the South. Its officers are: Adolph Boldt, secretary; C. G. Roussel, assistant secretary; C. C. Oden, traffic manager; Jerome H. Farbar, director of publicity. There are of course a great many businessmen who are heads of committees and good workers too, but the gentlemen named are the real workers and the ones who accomplish things.

The average citizen does not know how much good has been accomplished for Houston by the Chamber of Commerce, nor how much good is being planned for the future. It is a working body and it does not confine its labors to union hours of an eight hour day, but puts in every waking hour of the entire twenty-four. A vast amount of valuable information has been collected, and preserved in such form as to be immediately available.

Houston is today the home of vast commercial and manufacturing enterprises, most of them having come here during the last six or eight years. It is, for instance, the largest lumber market in the Southwest and one of the largest in the world. That does not mean that there are extensive mills and manufacturing plants here, but it does mean that about all the lumber made in Texas is controlled and handled by Houston firms, which are the greatest in the South. There are over 250 sawmills in Texas, Louisiana and Arkansas controlled and represented through offices located here. The following are the big Houston firms and the capacity of their plants:

Kirby Lumber Company, manufacturers, 400,000,000 feet.
Long-Bell Lumber Company, manufacturers, 500,000,000 feet.
West Lumber Company, manufacturers, 175,000,000 feet.
W. H. Norris Lumber Company, wholesalers, 100,000,000 feet.
Vaughan Lumber Company, wholesalers, 100,000,000 feet.
Continental Lumber and Tie Company, wholesalers, 100,000,000 feet.
Trinity River Lumber Company, manufacturers, 60,000,000 feet.
Central Coal and Coke Company, manufacturers, 50,000,000 feet.
W. T. Carter & Brother, manufacturers, 50,000,000 feet.
Carter Lumber Company, manufacturers, 40,000,000 feet.
W. R. Pickering Lumber Company, manufacturers, 50,000,000 feet.
Sabine Lumber Company, manufacturers, 40,000,000 feet.
Ray & Mihils, wholesalers, 40,000,000 feet.
Carter-Kelly Lumber Company, manufacturers, 30,000,000 feet.
Big Tree Lumber Co., manufacturers & wholesalers, 30,000,000 feet.
C. R. Cummings & Co., manufacturers, 25,000,000 feet.
J. S. and W. M. Rice, manufacturers, 25,000,000 feet.
Gebhart-Williams-Fenet, manufacturers, 25,000,000 feet.
Bland & Fisher, manufacturers, 25,000,000 feet.
J. C. Hill Lumber Company, manufacturers, 20,000,000 feet.
L. B. Manefee Lumber Company, manufacturers, 20,000,000 feet.
R. W. Wier Lumber Company, manufacturers, 20,000,000 feet.
Alf. Bennett Lumber Co., manufacturers & wholesalers, 20,000,000 ft.
R. C. Miller Lumber Company, manufacturers, 20,000,000 feet.
Bush Brothers, manufacturers, 15,000,000 feet.
Southern Pinery Tie & Lumber Co., manufacturers & wholesalers,
    10,000,000 feet.

The foregoing foot up within a fraction of two billion feet of lumber annually controlled by Houston firms.

Houston is the recognized center of all that relates to handling, refining, exporting and financing the output of the Texas oil fields and is rapidly assuming the same relation to the oil fields of Oklahoma. An idea of the importance of Houston in this respect may be formed from the fact that there are five large oil refineries here, thirteen oil dealers and thirty-nine producers and exporters, twenty-three of the latter being large concerns. Houston has the largest independent oil company in the United States, the Texas Company, with a capital of $86,000,000. Pipelines from all the Texas fields and from Oklahoma converge at Houston and additional lines, to cost in the neighborhood of $7,000,000, are being constructed.

Houston naturally holds first place as a rice market, since it has every possible advantage. Aside from the physical aspect, there is something of a sentimental side to the question, since it was a Houston man who first pointed out the possibilities of rice culture here and who actually undertook steps to develop it. The late J. R. Morris, as early as the middle seventies, organized a company and took out a charter for the purpose of cultivating rice in all that territory lying between Houston and the San Jacinto River. He had a survey made which demonstrated that Houston is about twenty-eight feet lower than some near point on the San Jacinto River from which he proposed to start his canal. He wanted to deflect the water from the river and use it in irrigating the prairie lands and to utilize the surplus in running machinery at the mouth of White Oak Bayou, at the foot of Main Street.

For some reason nothing was ever done by Mr. Morris and his associates, but attention was drawn to the possibilities of rice culture, which has resulted in its becoming one of the large and rapidly growing industries of Texas. At the time of Mr. Morris' death it is doubtful if there was as much as an acre of ground in Texas devoted to the cultivation of rice. Today rice holds third place in point of importance among the crops of the state. Harris County alone has 30,000 acres, while there are 253,560 acres in all, of which about 200,000 acres are tributary to Houston.

Houston has five rice mills with a daily capacity of 7,600 bags, while the capacity of all the mills in the state is 25,200 bags. The annual production averages about two and a quarter million bags, and Houston handles about three-fourths of it.

Including the railroad shop workers there are several thousand wage earners in Houston employed all the year round to whom is paid something like $8,500,000 annually. This is not for one year, but is for every year and therefore it is not surprising that Houston should be known as the best retail town in Texas. There are over twelve hundred retail dealers who, according to an estimate made by the Chamber of Commerce based on almost complete returns, do an annual business of $55,000,000.

The wholesale business of Houston is very great, estimated by the Chamber of Commerce at $90,000,000 annually. The leading articles and the amount of business done in each are as follows:

machinery, $3,000,000
hardware, $4,000,000
lumber, $35,000,000
petroleum products, $1,000,000
drugs and chemicals, $4,000,000
paints and glass, $1,000,000
furniture, $1,400,000
dry goods, $1,750,000
liquors, $1,250,000
beer and ice, $2,500,000
groceries, $8,000,000
produce, $4,600,000
sugar and molasses, $2,000,000
tobacco, $1,250,000
packing house products, $3,750,000

When to these is added the business done in building material, paving material, electrical supplies and other things, it becomes apparent that the estimate of $90,000,000 must be under rather than above the actual figures.

Not counting the railroads, trust companies and banks, there are 376 incorporated companies doing business in Houston, the combined capital of which is $145,943,900. There are, of course, thousands of individuals and numerous unincorporated companies doing business in addition to these, which shows the magnitude of Houston as a trade center.

In the early days the Houston merchants and property owners who wished to insure against fire loss were compelled to send to New Orleans for their policies, for there were no local insurance agents here. These conditions prevailed until 1858, when Mr. John Dickinson established the first agency in Houston, representing a New Orleans firm. Just about the time Mr. Dickinson got his office working satisfactorily and began doing a lucrative business, the war broke out and knocked his business into a cocked hat.

In 1868 the first local insurance company was organized in Houston. This was the Planters' Fire Insurance Company, which did a good business until 1880, when a disastrous cotton fire occurred, causing such heavy losses to the company that it went into voluntary liquidation.

In 1895 the Houston Fire and Marine Insurance Company was organized. This company did a good business for several years, but through the innocent purchase of a lot of bogus bonds, it was forced to suspend and go out of business a few years ago.

The Guarantee Life Insurance Company was the first life insurance company organized in Houston. It was organized in 1906 with a capital stock of $100,000 and prospered from the very beginning. It does an immense business and has over $13,000,000 insurance in force. The officers of the Guarantee are Jonathan Lane, president; John H. Thompson, vice president and Charles Boedeker, secretary-treasurer.

The Great Southern Life Insurance Company is, in some respects, a wonderful organization. It was organized in 1909 and though it is less than three years old, it has done and is still doing, an immense business. It has a capital of $500,000 and a surplus of $500,000 and outstanding insurance of over ten million dollars. Among its policyholders is one who is insured for $100,000, the largest policy ever written in Texas for one person. The officers of the Great Southern are J. S. Rice, president; O. S. Carlton, C. G. Pillot, J. S. Cullinan and P. H. McFadden of Beaumont, vice presidents; J. T. Scott, treasurer and Louis St. J. Thomas, secretary.

CHAPTER XIII:
SPEAK UP, HOUSTON

The *Houston Telegraph* of March 18, 1853, mentions the fact that some of the material for the telegraph line between Houston and Galveston had been received at the latter place. At that time the land part of the line had been constructed, but the two-mile stretch across the bay at Virginia Point was causing a great deal of trouble. Modern submarine cables were unknown at that time and many substitutes for them were suggested and tried. Finally the difficulty was overcome by using ordinary iron wire covered with gutta percha, which was warranted by its maker to last for one year and which cost $350 per mile. But before the problem was solved, the land part of the line grew old and fell down, so that it was not until 1858 that an actual working line was constructed between the two cities, this being the first telegraph line constructed in Texas. It was not a great financial undertaking, since the cost of the entire fifty miles including the two miles of bay, was only $6,200, of which the Houston people contributed $3,000.

Having constructed the Galveston-Houston line successfully, the owners formed a company called the Star State Telegraph Company and built a line along the Texas and New Orleans railroad which was being constructed about that time. When the war occurred, the company had its line completed to Orange in East Texas. As an item of interest, it may be stated here that when the Texas ports were blockaded during the war it was almost impossible to get sulfuric acid with which the batteries of those days were operated, and that telegraphing would have been impossible had not some genius found that the acid water from Sour Lake made an admirable substitute for sulfuric acid. The telegraph batteries were charged with Sour Lake water and all difficulty disappeared.

Soon after the close of the war, the Star State Company was absorbed by the Southwestern Telegraph Company which then covered most of the Southern States. Mr. D. P. Shepherd, who is possibly the oldest telegraph operator in this country and is said to have been the first operator in the world to take a message by ear, was placed in charge of the new telegraph company with headquarters in Houston.

In 1867 the Southwestern was absorbed by the Western Union Telegraph Company, the latter company gaining control of all the telegraph lines in the United States. The Western Union remained master of the field until late in 1910, when it, in turn, was absorbed by the Southwestern Telegraph and Telephone Company, the largest corporation of its kind in the world.

The first manager of the Western Union in Houston was Mr. Merrit Harris, who died during the great yellow fever epidemic of 1867 and was succeeded by Col. Phil Fall, who has the distinction of being the oldest operator in actual service in this country.

The Postal Telegraph Company opened its office in Houston during July, 1898. The establishment was merely on a small scale, but by strict attention to business has managed to build up an immense business and has made itself a formidable competitor of the Southwestern Telegraph and Telephone Company in the local field. The Postal aims at promptness and dispatch, and has thus earned an enviable reputation.

In the latter part of 1910 the Mackey Telegraph and Cable Company established its chief office in Houston, thus making Houston the great telegraph center of the state. All the companies have direct cable connection with all parts of the world, but the Mackey company has facilities possessed by no other company. The cable business out of Houston is immense and the general telegraphing done by all the Houston lines amounts to very near four million messages each year and is constantly increasing.

In the late seventies, the latest in communication invention arrived in Houston in the form of a telephone. The *Houston Telegram* of June 18, 1878 reports:

> Mr. J. W. Stacey, the efficient manager of the Western Union Telegraph office in this city, has procured a telephone of the latest improved construction, which he will put up for use during the military encampment of the volunteers of the State next week. The line will run from the Fair Grounds to Mr. G. W. Baldwin's library room in the Telegram building and everybody wishing to have the pleasure of conversing with a friend a mile distant will have an opportunity. Our friends from the country and many in the city who are skeptical about the truthful working of the wonderful instrument, will have an opportunity to test it to their satisfaction. To many of them it will be quite a curiosity, and we expect to see its capacity fully tried. Mr. Stacey will make a trial test today and will have the apparatus in perfect working order by the end of the week.

During the fall of the same year, Mr. Pendarvis, who was telegraph operator for the Morgan Transportation Company, connected his office in Houston with the office in Clinton, ten miles away and for a time had direct telephone connection between the two. Commenting on this innovation the *Houston Telegram* stated that unquestionably when the great convenience of the telephone was appreciated they would be installed in railroad depots, business houses and, perhaps, residences. This prediction has come true in a much greater degree than the *Telegram* supposed possible.

It was not until 1880 that a telephone exchange was established in Houston. Two years later Mr. G. W. Foster took charge of the exchange and it was largely through his efforts and the hearty and valuable assistance of his wife that the telephone business in Texas attained such huge proportions in so short a time. Mr. Foster is still an active man in the company and fills one of the higher offices. The local company has just completed its own skyscraper at a cost of about $1,000,000, and has equipment for caring for 20,000 subscribers with out making further additions to its plant.

Houston's long distance telephone system is very complete, with twelve circuits to Galveston, seven to Beaumont, three to San Antonio, three to Dallas and one each to Fort Worth and Corpus Christi. Each of these direct circuits has branch circuits reaching all parts of the state.

In addition to the old telephone company there is an automatic telephone company also operating in Houston. This company owns its own home, an elegant building on Rusk Avenue near the Federal building.

There are two wireless telegraph companies operating in Houston. One is a strictly private affair owned by the Texas Company. This company has 2,700 miles of private wires in Texas, Oklahoma and Kansas. It uses these wires for business purposes, but keeps its wireless plant always in readiness for use in case of failure of its wires. The company owns similar outfits at Beaumont and in Oklahoma.

The other company, the Texas Wireless Telegraph-Telephone, is the only one engaged in public and commercial business. The company has perfectly equipped stations at Houston, San Antonio, Victoria, Fredericksburg, Waco and Fort Worth. It is distinctly a home company, for all of its stock is owned by Texans, and its officers and managers are all Texans.

The Houston Electric Light Company was organized in 1882, by Mr. E. Raphael. Its first officers were: E. Raphael, president; D. F. Stuart, secretary. The board of trustees were: A. Grosebeck, B. A. Botts, F. A. Rice,

E. P. Hill, D. F. Stuart, J. C. Hutcherson, G. L. Porter and E. Raphael. At that time, only the old Brush carbon lights were used. Mr. Raphael exhibited the first incandescent lamp ever seen in Houston in August, 1883. The great merit of the incandescent lamp was recognized at once and Mr. Raphael secured a contract to equip the Howard Oil Mill plant with them. This was the first installation of incandescent electric lights in a building in Texas. Mr. Raphael and his associates conducted the business for a year or so and then sold their plant to the Houston Gas Company. That company organized the present electric light company in 1894.

CHAPTER XIV:
MR. RICE AND HIS INSTITUTE

Among the very early settlers in the new town of Houston was Mr. Wm. M. Rice, who was destined to impress his name indelibly on this, his adopted home. Mr. Rice was a remarkable man. He began his mercantile life in a modest way, but by strict attention to every detail of his business he was soon able to extend his field of operation. His success was assured from the beginning, and, his money-making instinct, or faculty, largely developed, he soon became one of the best known and most prosperous merchants of the city.

Much has been said and written about Mr. Rice. Some things absolutely true and some largely imaginative. Those who knew him are aware of the fact that he would not have appreciated some of the latter. Mr. Rice was intensely practical, and cared little for the applause of the crowd. He was a successful merchant, a king of finance and nothing more. He was absolutely honest and just, and what was more to the point, he was as just to himself as he was to others. If he made a contract he carried out every detail and he required those who made the other side to do the same. If he owed money he paid every cent of the debt and those who owed him money were required to settle in full. He was merely an ordinary merchant and businessman, though a remarkably successful one.

Had the early friends and associates of Mr. Rice been asked to select one of their number who would make a princely donation towards the cause of education, the chances are ten to one that Mr. Rice would never have been selected. If he ever gave a thought to art, science or literature no one knew of it. The first intimation that he took the least interest in educational matters was given some time during the middle eighties when the city was endeavoring to raise money to purchase what was known as Academy Square and the old building that stood on it, for the purpose of turning it into a high school. The property had been owned by a company but had passed into the hands of a private citizen and the city wanted to buy it. Mr. Rice was living in New York at the time, but was paying an annual visit to Houston when the purchase matter came up.

Mr. E. Raphael, who was very close to Mr. Rice, and who looked after some of his Houston interests for him, was requested by a committee of citizens to ask Mr. Rice for a subscription to the fund. Mr. Raphael did so and was met by a prompt refusal. Mr. Rice stated that it was the duty of the city and not of individuals to care for such things as public schools. Then he surprised Mr. Raphael by telling him that he was thinking of a plan by which he hoped to establish a great educational institution here. A few months later he took into his confidence a few gentlemen and, after a thorough discussion of his plans, an organization was formed and, in 1891, a charter was applied for and granted. The terms of the charter were most liberal and the trustees were given wide latitude for the future organization of a great nonpolitical, non-sectarian institution of technical learning to be dedicated to the advancement of letters, science and art, to be located in the adopted home of Mr. Rice. As a nucleus for the endowment fund, Mr. Rice placed in the hands of the trustees an interest-bearing note for $200,000.

The original trustees were the following named gentlemen: Mr. Rice, himself; his brother, Mr. F. A. Rice, Mr. A. S. Richardson, Mr. James A. Baker, Mr. J. E. McAshan, Mr. E. Raphael and Mr. C. M. Lombardi. Under the terms of the charter this board is made self-perpetuating and its members are elected for life. Since its organization vacancies have been filled by the selection of the following: Mr. Wm. M. Rice, Jr., a nephew of Mr. Rice, Mr. B. B. Rice and Dr. E. O. Lovett.

Having taken the first step, Mr. Rice became infatuated with the idea he had conceived, and from time to time, transferred to the trustees large interests and then, by his will, left the bulk of his large fortune to the institute. Mr. Rice was murdered in New York in 1900 and there was a long fight in court over his will.

When the trustees finally came into possession of the full resources of the foundation, which then amounted to approximately ten million dollars, they invited Dr. Edgar Odell Lovett, Professor at Princeton University, to assist them in formulating and executing the educational programme of the Institute. The President thereupon undertook a year's journey of study which extended from England to Japan. Upon the completion of this preliminary investigation by Dr. Lovett, a most suitable site of three hundred acres was secured. To Messrs. Cram, Goodhue and Ferguson of Boston was committed the task of designing a general architectural plan consistent with the programme which had been adopted for the Institute.

In 1911, on the seventy-fifth anniversary of Texan Independence, the cornerstone of the Administration Building was laid by the trustees. This building, together with the first wing of the Engineering Quadrangle, the

Mechanical Laboratory and Power House, and the first Residential Hall for Men, is rapidly nearing completion. The initial building schedule also includes special laboratories for instruction and investigation in physics, chemistry, and biology, and in the application of these sciences to the arts of industry and commerce. In the preparation of these preliminary laboratory plans the Institute has enjoyed the cooperation of an advisory committee consisting of Professor Ames, director of the physical laboratory of Johns Hopkins University; Professor Conklin, director of the biological laboratory of Princeton University; Professor Richards, chairman of the department of chemistry, Harvard University; and Professor Stratton, director of the National Bureau of Standards.

The academic work of the Institute will begin this autumn on the 23rd day of September. A few days later the formal opening will be observed with appropriate ceremonies of inauguration and dedication, on October 10th, 11th, and 12th, 1912. Distinguished scholars and scientists from a number of foreign seats of learning have consented to participate in the proceedings of the Institute's first academic festival by preparing lectures in the fundamental sciences of mathematics, physics, chemistry, and biology, and in the liberal humanities of philosophy, history, letters, and art.

The initial staff of the Institute will be organized in a faculty of science and a faculty of letters. Of those who have been selected for positions under the direction of the faculty of science it is possible to announce the following elections, in alphabetical order:

Philip Heckman Arbuckle, B. A. (Chicago), of Georgetown, Texas; Director of Athletics at Southwestern University; to be Instructor in Athletics.

Percy John Daniell, M. A. (Cambridge), of Liverpool, England; Senior Wrangler and Rayleigh Prizeman of the University of Cambridge; Lecturer in Mathematics at the University of Liverpool; to be Research Associate in Applied Mathematics.

William Franklin Edwards, B. Sc. (Michigan), of Houston, Texas; formerly Instructor in the University of Michigan, and later President of the University of Washington; to be Lecturer in Chemistry.

Griffith Conrad Evans, Ph. D. (Harvard), of Rome, Italy; Sheldon Fellow of Harvard University ; to be Asst. Professor of Pure Mathematics.

Julian Sorrell Huxley, M. A. (Oxford), of Oxford, England; Newdigate Prizeman of the University of Oxford; Lecturer in Biology at Balliol College, and Inter-collegiate Lecturer in Oxford University; to be Research Associate in Biology.

Francis Ellis Johnson, B. A., E. E. (Wisconsin), of Houston, Texas; recently with the British Columbia Electric Railway Company; to be Instructor in Electrical Engineering.

Edgar Odell Lovett, Ph. D. (Virginia and Leipsic), LL. D. (Drake and Tulane), of Houston, Texas; formerly Professor of Mathematics in Princeton University, and later Head of the Department of Astronomy in the same institution; President of the Institute; to be Professor of Mathematics.

William Ward Watkin, B. Sc. (Pennsylvania), Architect, of Houston, Texas; to be Instructor in Architectural Engineering.

Harold Albert Wilson, F. R. S., D. Sc. (Cambridge), of Montreal, Canada; Fellow of Trinity College, Cambridge University; formerly Professor in King's College, London; Research Professor in McGill University; to be Professor of Physics.

There is being constituted a faculty of letters in which will be developed facilities for elementary and advanced courses in the so-called humanities, thereby enabling the Institute to offer both the advantages of a liberal general education and those of special and professional training. For these faculties of science and letters the best available instructors and investigators are being sought in the hope of assembling in Houston a group of unusually able scientists and scholars through whose productive work the new university should speedily take a place of considerable importance among the established institutions of the country.

The subjects in which instruction will be provided as rapidly as possible are mathematics, physics, chemistry, biology, engineering, architecture, ancient languages, modern languages, history and politics, philosophy and psychology, economics and sociology, and art and archaeology. The programmes of study are being so arranged as to offer a variety of courses leading after four years of undergraduate work to bachelor's degrees in arts, in science, in letters, and in their applications to the several fields of engineering, domestic arts, and other regions of applied science. Extensive general courses in the various domains of scientific knowledge will be available but in the main, the programmes will consist of subjects carefully coordinated and calling for considerable concentration of study. For the advanced degrees, Master of Arts, Doctor of Philosophy, and Doctor of Engineering, every facility will be afforded properly qualified graduate students to undertake lines of study and research under the direction of the Institute's resident and visiting professors.

Candidates for admission to the Institute who present satisfactory testimonials as to their character will be accepted either upon successful examination in the entrance subjects or by certificate of graduation from an accredited public or private high school.

There will be no charge for tuition and no fees for registration or examination in the Institute. A small deposit will be required to cover possible breakage in the laboratories and losses from the libraries; the balance from this contingent fee is, of course, returnable at the close of the session.

Rooms in the Residential Hall, for men, completely furnished exclusive of linen, together with table board at the Institute Commons, will be available for from eighteen to twenty dollars per month of four weeks. For both single and double rooms the rental will be uniform without regard to their location, and they will be let in the order of applications received. Diagrams showing the floor plans will be sent on request to anyone who may be interested. Accommodations for the residence of young women on the university grounds will not be offered during the coming year. The Residential Hall for Men is of absolutely fireproof construction, heated by steam, lighted by electricity, cleaned by vacuum apparatus, and equipped with the most approved forms of sanitary plumbing, providing adequate bathing facilities on every floor.

The general plan for the improvement of the site of the Institute calls for a number of playing and exhibition fields in the vicinity of the residential groups. In fact the wide expanse of the campus affords abundant space for every variety of physical exercise. A determined effort will be made to systematize and make general a sane devotion to outdoor sports in climatic conditions, which render athletics and open-air gymnastics profitably possible the whole year round. The daily timetable of each student will include a definite period under the instructor in athletics. Similarly, with a view to developing every student in the manly art of self-defense in oratory and disputation there have been appointed, in the South Tower of the first Residential Hall for Men, halls for two literary and debating societies, whose activities should supplement the work of certain chairs under the faculty of letters.